Hamlet

ARDEN STUDENT SKILLS: LANGUAGE AND WRITING

Series Editor:

Dympna Callaghan, Syracuse University

Published Titles

The Tempest, Brinda Charry
Macbeth, Emma Smith
Romeo and Juliet, Catherine Belsey
Othello, Laurie Maguire
Twelfth Night, Frances E. Dolan

Forthcoming Titles

Antony and Cleopatra, Virginia Mason Vaughan
King Lear, Jean Howard
A Midsummer Night's Dream, Heidi Brayman Hackel
The Merchant of Venice, Douglas Lanier
Much Ado About Nothing, Indira Ghose

Hamlet

Language and Writing

DYMPNA CALLAGHAN

Bloomsbury Arden Shakespeare
An imprint of Bloomsbury Publishing Plc

B L O O M S B U R Y
LONDON • NEW DELHI • NEW YORK • SYDNEY

Bloomsbury Arden Shakespeare

An imprint of Bloomsbury Publishing Plc

Imprint previously known as The Arden Shakespeare

50 Bedford Square	1385 Broadway
London	New York
WC1B 3DP	NY 10018
UK	USA

www.bloomsbury.com

BLOOMSBURY, THE ARDEN SHAKESPEARE and the Diana logo are trademarks of Bloomsbury Publishing Plc

First published 2015

© Dympna Callaghan, 2015

Dympna Callaghan has asserted her right under the Copyright, Designs and Patents Act, 1988, to be identified as author of this work.

British Library Cataloguing-in-Publication Data
A catalogue record for this book is available from the British Library.

ISBN: HB: 978-1-4725-2028-9
PB: 978-1-4081-5489-2
ePDF: 978-1-4742-1604-3
ePub: 978-1-4742-1603-6

Library of Congress Cataloging-in-Publication Data
Callaghan, Dympna.
Hamlet : language and writing / Dympna Callaghan.
pages cm.-- (Arden student guides)
Includes bibliographical references.
ISBN 978-1-4081-5489-2 (paperback)-- ISBN 978-1-4725-2028-9 (hardback)
1. Shakespeare, William, 1564-1616. Hamlet. 2. Shakespeare, William,
1564-1616--Characters--Hamlet. 3. Shakespeare, William, 1564-1616--Language. I. Title.
PR2807.C245 2015
822.3'3--dc23
2014037431

Typeset by Fakenham Prepress Solutions, Fakenham, Norfolk NR21 8NN
Printed and bound in Great Britain

CONTENTS

ACKNOWLEDGEMENTS

I am grateful to Frances E. Dolan, Carol Faulkner and Musa Gurnis for their astute responses to various queries during the course of my work on *Hamlet: Language and Writing*. I have also been particularly fortunate to have the immensely gifted Amy Burnette as my graduate assistant throughout this process. Discussing *Hamlet* with Amy has been one of the joys of writing this book, and she has responded to every page of it. My husband, Chris R. Kyle, shared his immense knowledge of early modern English history on more occasions than I can count. I am also grateful to my wonderful editor at Arden, Margaret Bartley, and to her assistant, Emily Hockley. They have been a pleasure to work with. Most of all, I want to thank my students, past and present, in ETS 121: 'Introduction to Shakespeare' at Syracuse University for their intellectual curiosity about *Hamlet*. This book is dedicated to them.

Throughout the book, all quotations from early modern plays refer to current Arden editions unless otherwise noted, and also unless otherwise noted, biblical quotations refer to the 1560 edition of the Geneva Bible (available online). I have modernized most of the quotations from early modern sources except where it seemed important to represent the cadences of Elizabethan English more fully.

SERIES EDITOR'S PREFACE

This series puts the pedagogical expertise of distinguished literary critics at the disposal of students embarking upon Shakespeare Studies at university. While they demonstrate a variety of approaches to the plays, all the contributors to the series share a deep commitment to teaching and a wealth of knowledge about the culture and history of Shakespeare's England. The approach of each of the volumes is direct yet intellectually sophisticated and tackles the challenges Shakespeare presents. These volumes do not provide a shortcut to Shakespeare's works but instead offer a careful explication of them directed towards students' own processing and interpretation of the plays and poems.

Students' needs in relation to Shakespeare revolve overwhelmingly around language, and Shakespeare's language is what most distinguishes him from his rivals and collaborators – as well as what most embeds him in his own historical moment. The *Language and Writing* series understands language as the very heart of Shakespeare's literary achievement rather than as an obstacle to be circumvented. This series addresses the difficulties often encountered in reading Shakespeare alongside the necessity of writing papers for university examinations and course assessment. The primary objective here is to foster rigorous critical engagement with the texts by helping students develop their own critical writing skills. *Language and Writing* titles demonstrate how to develop students' own capacity to articulate and enlarge upon their experience of encountering the text, far beyond summarizing, paraphrasing or 'translating' Shakespeare's language into a more palatable, contemporary form. Each of the volumes in the series introduces the text as an act of specifically literary language and shows that the multifarious issues of life and history that Shakespeare's work addresses cannot be separated from their expression in language. In addition, each book takes students through a series of guidelines about how to develop viable undergraduate critical essays on the text in question, not by delivering interpretations, but rather by taking readers step-by-step through the process of discovering and developing their own critical ideas.

All the books include chapters examining the text from the point of view of its composition, that is, from the perspective of Shakespeare's own process of composition as a reader, thinker and writer. The opening chapters consider when and how the play was written, addressing, for example, the extant literary and cultural acts of language, from which Shakespeare constructed his work – including his sources – as well as the generic, literary and theatrical conventions at his disposal. Subsequent sections demonstrate how to engage in detailed examination and analysis of the text and focus on the literary, technical and historical intricacies of Shakespeare's verse and prose. Each volume also includes some discussion of performance. Other chapters cover textual issues as well as the interpretation of the extant texts for any given play on stage and screen, treating for example, the use of stage directions or parts of the play that are typically cut in performance. Authors also address issues of stage/film history as they relate to the cultural evolution of Shakespeare's words. In addition, these chapters deal with the critical reception of the work, particularly the newer theoretical and historicist approaches that have revolutionized our understanding of Shakespeare's language over the past 40 years. Crucially, every chapter contains a section on 'Writing matters', which links the analysis of Shakespeare's language with students' own critical writing.

The series empowers students to read and write about Shakespeare with scholarly confidence and hopes to inspire their enthusiasm for doing so. The authors in this series have been selected because they combine scholarly distinction with outstanding teaching skills. Each book exposes the reader to an eminent scholar's teaching in action and expresses a vocational commitment to making Shakespeare accessible to a new generation of student readers.

Professor Dympna Callaghan
Series Editor
Arden Student Skills: Language and Writing

PREFACE

By the time he wrote *Hamlet*, Shakespeare was a seasoned poet and dramatist, the author of approximately 21 plays and two long poems, among other works. Yet, the play represents a milestone both in the English language and in Shakespeare's career as a writer, introducing, by some estimates, over 600 words that were either completely new in Shakespeare's usage or else, in the case of approximately 170 words, the first recorded usage in English itself. Shakespeare's capacity for linguistic and poetic invention reached new heights with the composition of this play. Its innovations are not only those of vocabulary, but also – supremely – in the play's representation of character. Yet, there are many ways in which *Hamlet* is not about novelty and originality. As was his ordinary working procedure, Shakespeare was using an existing story, in this case one from Danish history that had already seen theatrical presentation before he wrote the play. Although *Hamlet* represents a radical reworking of the Danish tale, Shakespeare's basic framework for this play was the well-established genre of revenge tragedy, and an earlier version of the play, most likely written by someone else, was already familiar to his audiences. The focus of this volume will be on Shakespeare's writing because it is this that makes *Hamlet* an extraordinary play.

From your point of view as a student, writing about *Hamlet* may seem overwhelming in the face of all that has already been written. In doing so, however, you will be participating in an ongoing cultural conversation. You and your generation have a unique contribution to make to this discussion, and that's important because *Hamlet* is about the Big Picture – sex, love, life, death and meaning – and is in an aesthetic form, tragedy, that was specifically designed to address it. The play concerns the moral ambiguities that confront anyone taking action in the world, and these must be faced afresh by every new generation: your time has come.

In a sense, too, the very same challenges that Shakespeare encountered as a writer – how to be innovative with established material – also confront you as a student: how to write about *Hamlet* in face of the uneasy feeling that 'it's all been said before'. Yet, the challenge of making it new with old material is not only what makes Shakespeare's *Hamlet Hamlet*, but also what constitutes the Renaissance itself – the rebirth and flowering of art and culture of which *Hamlet* is such an important part. It was by negotiating this tension between what had been said before in the languages of the ancient world, classical Greek and Latin, and the opportunities for new literary invention in still-spoken languages, European vernaculars, that Renaissance humanism ultimately gave rise to some of the greatest works in world literature, including those of Shakespeare.

How to use this book

You can read this book from start to finish, or you can start reading any of the five main chapters depending on your immediate needs or interests. Further subheadings of each relatively self-contained unit of the chapters will help you to hone in on a particular issue and will assist you in addressing or resolving problems you may confront as you are reading the play. Throughout the book, the emphasis will be on detailed engagement with Shakespeare's words. This book begins by addressing some of the problems you might encounter in reading *Hamlet*. In addition, the Introduction explains Shakespeare's development as a writer up to and beyond the time he composed *Hamlet* as well as offering some context for the play in terms of his thematic preoccupations and his writing style. The last part of the Introduction offers a broad overview of some of the many interpretations of the play as a way of helping you situate your own views and critical approaches.

Chapter One starts by looking at the most basic problem we face as readers in relation to Hamlet – namely, which of the three surviving texts of the play we should read. As we consider this question and how it arose in the first place, we will discover some of the key components of Shakespeare's own writing practices. This chapter compares and contrasts passages from different versions of the play and asks what these differences mean for our understanding of the distinctiveness of Shakespeare's language. Finally, this chapter examines revenge as the structure and framework for the tragic language of the play.

Chapter Two addresses both Shakespeare's use of language in *Hamlet* as well as his preoccupation with the idea of language (or, perhaps more accurately, language as an idea) and the ways in which he repeatedly draws our attention to 'Words, words, words' (2.2.188). Soliloquies, asides, letters, blank verse, prose, wordplay and rhetoric are all ways of shaping and manipulating language that Shakespeare used to dramatic effect.

Chapter Three asks why *Hamlet* represents such a watershed in theatre history and how engagement with the play has changed over the course of the centuries since it was written. Of perennial concern, for example, is the issue of Hamlet's character; however since the late twentieth century, questions about why he so despises women have become increasingly prominent. This chapter also examines historical aspects of the play that were particularly significant at the time Shakespeare was writing. These include philosophical ideas, such as scepticism, the notion of melancholy, the role of women in society and political ideas about power and just government.

The final portions of the Introduction and of Chapters One through Three are devoted to 'writing matters'. These sections are designed to help you develop the confidence and skill to write effectively and eloquently about Shakespeare. As you may have heard, 'writing is thinking', and some of the exercises will encourage you to think creatively, to draw outside the lines, so to speak. You will learn to read closely and in detail as well as how to step back and integrate your close readings with a more comprehensive view of the play. Doing this, you will discover that you really do have something to say about *Hamlet* and that you are able to generate new ideas when you move away from the sometimes rigid patterns of writing and thinking that we tend to associate with formal papers and exams. That said, all the writing exercises in this book culminate in Chapter Four, which is precisely about how to approach examinations and formal course papers. If you have completed many of the previous exercises, by Chapter Four, you will find yourself ready to write a longer essay or term paper assignment. My hope is that you will really enjoy this stage of the writing process and will, despite the hard work involved (and hard work is a key ingredient) have a real sense of accomplishment when you submit your assignment.

A note on editions

The edition of *Hamlet* used throughout this book is The Arden Shakespeare *Hamlet* edited by Ann Thompson and Neil Taylor (2006).

Hamlet has become part of the language. It is unquestionably the most canonical text of English literature and, as such, we have a sense of its solidity and weight. Yet, in many ways this is one of the most fundamental misapprehensions about the play. A literary monument it may be, but that there are no fewer than three surviving versions of *Hamlet* makes it one of the most complex and unstable texts in the canon of Shakespeare's works. What we usually mean when we refer to *Hamlet* is a conflated version of the texts that we have inherited – in other words, an editorial amalgamation of at least two, and sometimes of all three, surviving texts. This presents a problem because whatever we may say about a conflated text, it is certainly not what Shakespeare wrote. We do not in fact know whether he wrote many of the lines that appear in the very first printed version of the play. The issue is so complicated that the Arden editors of *Hamlet* decided to present all three versions of the text. We will discuss the challenges presented by these multiple texts in more detail in Chapter One, but for now, it is enough to note that the first volume of the Arden *Hamlet*, our main text, is an edited version based on the play that was published in 1604–5. So, from a practical standpoint, if you are using a different edition, you may have a very different reference or even need to consult the appendix at the back of your edition where major textual variants are often printed. The most important thing to grasp from the point of view of studying the play, however, is that, even though we may pretend otherwise, there is no single, authentic *Hamlet*.

Introduction

Hamlet is intimidating. We often worry about actually reading the play because we have inherited the idea of the play's greatness, and it looms over us like some great monument. The nineteenth-century English poet Alfred Lord Tennyson said the play was 'the greatest creation in literature' (Tandon, 201), and Ernest Jones summed up the cultural appraisal of *Hamlet* very precisely when he wrote that the play 'is almost universally considered to be the chief masterpiece of one of the greatest minds the world has known' (Jones, 24). It is not that these are erroneous ideas – *Hamlet* is a great play – but it is not your job in writing about it to come up with even more ways to say that. Your task is to engage with the play, and in order to do that you need to put ideas about greatness aside. The play is a lot less daunting (and much more exciting) than some of the deadening, grandiose things that have been written about it. You will be on the right track if you keep remembering what Hamlet said: 'The play's the thing' (2.2.539).

*

Given the choice, most young people would rather read a funny, sexy poem than *Hamlet*. This is not my opinion. It is that of one of Shakespeare's contemporaries, Gabriel Harvey, who in 1598 wrote the earliest account that has come down to us of Shakespeare's most famous play: 'The younger sort takes much delight in Shakespeare's Venus & Adonis: but … his tragedie of Hamlet, prince of Denmarke … please[s] the wiser sort' (Thompson and Taylor, 47). The glittering humorous eroticism of Shakespeare's narrative poem, *Venus and Adonis* (1593), according to Harvey, appeals to the youth much more than the serious profundity of Shakespeare's tragic masterpiece. Now, we might take issue with Harvey's belief that in order to appreciate *Hamlet* you have to be old and wise, especially since it sounds so close to that 'intruding fool' Polonius' pronouncement that, '[I]t is common for the younger sort / To lack discretion' (2.1.113–14). What is interesting, and perhaps comforting, about Harvey's remark, however, is that even in Elizabethan England, tragedy was clearly understood to be harder to comprehend and less accessible to audiences of both readers and playgoers.

Shakespeare seems to have known that he had written a play that at least some members of his audience would find difficult to understand. Hamlet's instructions to the Players who arrive in Elsinore direct the audience's attention to this very fact. The best theatre, Hamlet says, forgoes popular approval and is 'caviare to the general' [the general public]' (2.2.374–5), a delicacy that only the initiated could appreciate, appealing instead to only judicious, discerning spectators. This is not to say, however, that *Hamlet* was written only for people who liked difficult ideas. Theatregoers in Shakespeare's time constituted a much broader spectrum of the population than is true today, and we know that Shakespeare himself was invested quite literally and financially (as he was a shareholder in his company) in appealing to all social and intellectual levels of his audience. Thus, some elements of *Hamlet* are as rooted in folk culture as they are in, say, classical literature. Even though the play's deep philosophical themes make it potentially daunting, the Ghost and the suspense generated by its appearance would have captured the attention of everybody in the playhouse – not just the educated elite.

However, anyone who has missed the last train home after a performance knows *Hamlet* is also long – Shakespeare's longest play, in fact. *Hamlet*, then, is not an easy play and, clearly, judging from Gabriel Harvey's comment, it is not only the passage of time that has made it thus. *Hamlet* makes us ask some of the hardest, most fundamental questions about human existence and mortality, and those questions, if they are not to become trite, require sophisticated and subtle expression. The aim of this book is to acknowledge some of the obstacles you might encounter in studying the play and to help you develop the critical skills to overcome them. You are learning to become a discerning reader capable of making your own arguments about *Hamlet* and you are developing the capacity to articulate those ideas in your own writing.

Language

The main idea that you should take away from this book is that the great innovation of *Hamlet*, and what makes it a watershed in Shakespeare's career, is the language of the play itself. The way to access that language is to resist temptations to speed-read your way through the play or to head to the Internet for a plot summary. Instead, slow down: focus, line-by-line, word-by-word, on what Shakespeare has written. The writer Francine Prose offers some wise advice about this process:

> [I]t's essential to slow down and read every word. Because one important thing that can be learned by reading slowly is the seemingly obvious but oddly underappreciated fact that language is the medium we use in much the same way a composer uses notes, the way a painter uses paint. I realize it may seem obvious, but it's surprising how easily we lose sight of the fact that words are the raw material out of which literature is crafted.
>
> Every page was once a blank page, just as every word that appears on it now was not always there, but instead reflects the final result of countless large and small deliberations. All the elements of good writing depend on the writer's skill in choosing one word instead of another. And what grabs and keeps our interest has everything to do with those choices. (Prose, 16)

Language, of course, is not an abstract entity. If it were, it would be incomprehensible. Rather, Shakespeare's language has recognizable roots in the time and place in which it was written, even as it succeeds in speaking to us with such force and passion down the centuries. Most of all, the language of the play is the vehicle through which Shakespeare creates his characters as well as the tragic predicament in which they find themselves. It is through language that he makes characters seem real and come alive on the stage. Indeed, in *Hamlet* Shakespeare creates these vivid impressions in a fashion that had not hitherto been achieved in English drama. As countless generations of readers and audiences have noticed, although Hamlet is not a real person, he really, really seems like one. As the great Romantic critic William Hazlitt put it in *Characters of Shakespeare's Plays* (1817), 'The character of Hamlet is itself a pure effusion of genius. It is not a character marked by strength of will or even of passion, but by refinement of thought and sentiment' (106). Whether or not we agree with Hazlitt's assessment (and we might not!), the point is that Hamlet's characterization is unique and that Shakespeare succeeds in creating the illusion of a three-dimensional being in a way that represents a milestone in drama.

The German philosopher Georg Wilhelm Hegel (1770–1831) argued that all tragedy was about conflict. In ancient Greek tragedy, incompatible demands were placed on the hero who was a flat character 'type', whereas in Shakespeare's great tragedies, the hero is a rounded 'individual'. For Hegel, in post-classical tragedy, the conflict was between the tragic individual, who is unique and specific, and the society that invariably tends toward conformity and is inimical to individuality. Not surprisingly, for Hegel, in modern tragedy (by which he simply meant 'not ancient'), 'soaring above the rest at an almost unapproachable height, stands Shakespeare' (qtd. in Paolucci, 219).

In tragedy, the pressure to make meaning in relation to life circumstances is exacerbated to the point of crisis so that the language in which this predicament is expressed needs to be compelling yet plausible and suited to the tragic dilemma that the play describes. Because the language of Hamlet is so powerful, many of the lines have become cultural clichés – they seem apposite to a great number of life's predicaments. The old joke about *Hamlet* is that it would be a great play if it didn't have so many quotations. That is, many of the lines, especially, 'To be, or not to be' (3.1.55) and 'Alas, poor Yorick' (5.1.174), are so culturally ubiquitous that when we watch and read the play itself, we feel as if these lines have had prior lives in some location other than Shakespeare's play.

Paradoxically, this cultural familiarity is accompanied by the belief that the language of the play itself is more or less incomprehensible and needs to be 'translated' into modern idiom. What such 'translations' do, however, is create an ingrained sense of helplessness in the face of the play itself. They also defer critical engagement with the text and inhibit direct access to it. This is not to deny that we may well wonder what some of the less-often-quoted expressions in the play mean – 'he galls his kibe' (5.1.133), for instance. The meaning of such terms is not readily apparent to the modern reader, but glosses to such archaic words are to be found at the bottom of the page of almost every available contemporary edition of the play. The Arden edition, for example, glosses this line as 'rubs against the sore on his heel' (Thompson and Taylor, 419). The distinction between a textual gloss and a 'translation' is that a gloss offers an explanation of a given word or phrase, whereas a so-called 'translation' claims to rewrite the entire text in a completely different language. You should not expect to read Shakespeare as easily and fluently as you might expect to read your favourite celebrity's Twitter posts, but Shakespeare's English is not a foreign language, and careful, persistent attention to the text will yield understanding of it.

Hamlet in Shakespeare's career

As with most of Shakespeare's plays, we do not know exactly when *Hamlet* was written. Most scholars date it around the turn of the century, 1600, about three years before the death of Queen Elizabeth I. Up to this point in his career, Shakespeare's accomplishments included a series of immensely successful English history plays, two remarkable long poems, the aforementioned *Venus and Adonis*, along with *The Rape of Lucrece*, most of his comedies, including the dazzlingly festive comedies *Twelfth Night* and *As You Like It*, and political drama in the form of the great Roman history play, *Julius Caesar*. *Hamlet* is the first of Shakespeare's four great tragedies, which include *Macbeth*, *King Lear*, and *Othello*. These plays focus on the downfall of their respective eponymous tragic heroes – that is, the characters from which the plays' titles are derived. These four plays are probably the most formidable literary monuments in the Western canon. *Hamlet* is arguably the greatest of these, though in later twentieth-century criticism, the bleak agnosticism of *King Lear* appealed to more modern, secular interests and began to rival *Hamlet* for pre-eminence among Shakespeare's works.

While the tragedies are each quite distinct from one another, there are important points of connection between them. Just as *Hamlet* concerns a father-son relationship and the relationship between the two brothers King Hamlet and Claudius, *Lear* is a play about an ageing father and his daughters and their fraught relationships with one another. In *Macbeth*, regicide manifests in the murder of Duncan, the king of Scotland, and ignites the plot, whereas in *Hamlet* regicide instigates, ironically, the hero's delay, even though he has sworn to the Ghost that he will take revenge. In both plays, supernatural forces are at work – the witches in *Macbeth* and the Ghost in *Hamlet*. The witches, or the 'Weird Sisters' (4.1.136), have the prophetic power to speak about what is to come, whereas *Hamlet*'s Ghost is devoid of all foreknowledge and speaks only about the past. Macbeth is easily incited to act even despite the fact that the witches offer him no direction as to how to proceed, leaving him with only the prediction that he will be king. He considers the possibility of letting events unfold without trying to manipulate outcomes: 'If Chance will have me King, why, Chance may crown me, Without my stir' (1.3.144). Finding himself unable to submit to the natural course of events, in killing the king he commits what was considered to be the most heinous crime of the early modern world. Paradoxically, Macbeth's struggle to control his fate succeeds only in sealing his tragic destiny. Hamlet, in contrast, is given very specific instructions by the Ghost but, unlike Macbeth, he fears making a compact with evil as he considers the consequences of taking the vengeance it commands: 'And shall I couple hell?' (1.5.93). He proves reluctant to avenge his father's murder, and the play is structured around both the Ghost's command in Act 1, '–Revenge his foul and most unnatural murder!' (1.5.25), and Hamlet's execution of that order at the very end of the play.

Like Hamlet, Othello has to be persuaded to take revenge upon his wife, Desdemona, for her alleged infidelity. Because his wife is completely innocent, Othello's downfall is that he kills her. More than the other three plays, *Othello* poignantly depicts the tragedy that is arguably inherent in the relationship between the sexes in the profoundly patriarchal world of early modern Europe. Othello's turn to sexual violence is strongly reminiscent of Hamlet's verbally abusive treatment of Ophelia and, arguably, of his mother. Perhaps even more surprising is that, of the four great tragedies, only *Othello* is based on a work of imaginative literature (an Italian novella) as opposed to a historical source. *Hamlet*, *Lear* and *Macbeth* are all based on chronicle histories and retell events that shaped medieval Denmark, ancient Britain, and medieval Scotland, respectively.

The basic outline of *Hamlet* derives from a story written in Latin by the medieval historian, Saxo Grammaticus (c. 1200), but which was printed in Paris in the sixteenth century as *Danorum Regum heroumque Historiae* (1514), while a different version was published in French in a collection of stories called *Histoires tragiques* (1570) by François de Belleforest. Despite using different names, *Hamlet* shares the general outlines of these accounts of the story. Crucial differences, however, are that, for example, in these treatments of the story there is no ghost. Even more importantly, in Saxo the Hamlet figure (who is called Amleth) emerges victorious by means of vengeance, and there is, therefore, no tragic ending to this thread of his story. In contrast, it goes without saying that *The Tragedy of Hamlet* poses a clear, dramatic designation: Hamlet won't come out of this alive.

Significantly, too, in both Belleforest and Saxo, it is no secret that the king has murdered his brother. In Belleforest, the Prince's mother is clearly guilty of adultery, having been seduced by the Claudius figure, Fengon, even before her husband was killed. In Shakespeare, whether or not Gertrude is guilty of adultery and whether she has conspired with Claudius in the murder of Hamlet's father remain two of the greatest puzzles of the play. When Hamlet discovers that his father did not die from natural causes but was actually murdered by his own brother, the Ghost of King Hamlet who delivers this intelligence demands revenge but, nonetheless, refuses to tell Hamlet whether his mother was party to his death. Despite the uncertainty on this count, Hamlet develops an obsession with the moral fallibility of women, not only of his mother but of Ophelia as well.

Throughout Shakespeare's career, from his very first, immensely popular history plays, the three parts of *Henry VI*, up until his retirement from the theatre, he considered what qualities of personality and what historical dynamics would endow certain of his characters with leadership skills while endowing others with characteristics that would render them incapable of seizing or maintaining power. Shakespeare's history plays especially reflect upon the role social and cultural forces play in either denying or granting political sovereignty to a specific individual. Crucially, the early histories dramatize the question of whether there is ever any justification for challenging the power of an anointed monarch. *Richard II* showed a weak king deposed by the usurper, Bolingbroke, who went on to become King Henry IV, while in *Richard III*, Shakespeare depicted his title character as a scheming Machiavel who murdered his way to the crown only to be killed in battle. Richard III's vanquisher was Henry Tudor, the future Henry VII, grandfather of Queen Elizabeth I, who was on the throne for most of Shakespeare's lifetime. Who and what conferred power and how that power was transmitted from one ruler to another were particularly vexed issues during that period because the ageing Elizabeth I had no direct heirs and had not named a successor. Even though Elizabeth herself did everything she could to quash it, this succession crisis was an obsessive theme of late sixteenth-century political debate. Thus, for most of his career, Shakespeare had been staging many of the same political issues that inform *Hamlet*, and appropriately so, since they were some of the biggest and most challenging questions of his time. As we shall see in the subsequent chapters, with *Hamlet*, we are left to wonder whether Hamlet himself should have inherited the crown upon his father's death, or whether we are supposed to understand Denmark as having a different model of succession.

Importantly, the major political themes that Shakespeare addressed were not confined to his tragedies and histories. In one of Shakespeare's greatest comedies, *As You Like It* (c. 1599), the usurped ruler, Duke Senior, survives in exile where he and his courtiers dwell like Robin Hood in the forest of Arden. Similarly, in *The Tempest* (c. 1611), one of Shakespeare's last plays, Prospero and his daughter live in exile on an island with only one other human inhabitant. The survival of these deposed rulers is, in comedy and in romance, a prelude to their restoration. In other genres, however, former sovereigns may appear as ghosts (even Lear is, metaphorically speaking, a ghost of his former self), as reminders of the ineradicable traces of lost power. The ghost of the dead ruler is presented onstage in both *Julius Caesar* and *Hamlet*; the ghosts of Richard III's murdered victims visit him at the Battle of Bosworth. These supernatural visitations are emblems of the transition into a new political order, and the ghosts are liminal figures whose temporal powers have been violently curtailed. They serve as metaphysical points of contact between the old regime and the new. In *Julius Caesar*, Caesar's corpse, bearing the stab wounds of his conspirators, is on display for the audience to see while his ghost looks on. In contrast, we do not actually see the body of King Hamlet onstage, but the story of his murder is both reported by his Ghost and then re-enacted in the play-within-the-play.

That *Hamlet* opens with the threat of a Norwegian invasion by Fortinbras, the nephew of the Norwegian king, and ends with him marching onstage to assume the throne as Denmark's new monarch also works to place the revenge plot within a much broader political context. Conventional scholarly wisdom has it that the play was written immediately following the Roman tragedy, *Julius Caesar* (1599), which concerns what was arguably regarded in Shakespeare's time as the most significant political event in all of history. *Hamlet* is about killing a king and *Julius Caesar* is about killing Caesar because he wants to become a king, a situation that would have spelled the end of the Roman republic. Both plays, in other words, are meditations on the relationship between legitimate and illegitimate forms of governance. Many of the characters in *Hamlet* are given decidedly Roman names – Horatio, Marcellus, Claudius, Laertes – and the play makes a number of direct references to Julius Caesar. Polonius tells us that he played in a dramatic adaptation of Caesar's assassination while he was a student at university: 'I was killed i'th' Capitol. Brutus killed me' (3.2.99–100). This statement serves to prefigure Hamlet's botched revenge attempt when he stabs Polonius through the tapestry (the arras) in the mistaken belief that his uncle Claudius is hiding there. Then, of course, Polonius' murder ignites another trajectory of revenge when Ophelia's brother, Laertes, vows to kill Hamlet. At this point, Claudius becomes sufficiently nervous to the point that he sends Hamlet to England where he has arranged to have him executed, and it is only because Hamlet uncovers the plot and escapes while at sea that he can return to Denmark and take revenge in Act 5 where, in the midst of poisons and rapiers, he finally kills Claudius. Yet, Shakespeare keeps forcefully reminding us of the political precedent for the murders in Elsinore. Indeed, at the beginning of the play, the supernatural events that transpire are likened by Hamlet's friend, Horatio, to those 'In the most high and palmy state of Rome' (1.1.112) – when graves regurgitate their dead to forewarn of Caesar's murder. At the end of the play, Horatio forges another direct connection with Julius Caesar when he tells the dying Hamlet that he feels it would be more honourable to kill himself than to continue to live: 'I am more an antique Roman than a Dane' (5.2.325). The ancient Romans viewed suicide as an honourable and heroic death, or what Shakespeare refers to in *Antony and Cleopatra* as 'the high Roman Fashion' (4.15.91), which sharply contrasts with subsequent Judeo-Christian cultures. These dimensions of *Hamlet* may seem rather surprising because so many productions of the play focus on the decidedly personal and familial aspects of Hamlet's tragedy – his father's murder at the hand of his uncle, his mother's remarriage to his father's killer – rather than on the public and political dimensions of the play, especially the question of whether Hamlet is the rightful heir to his father's kingdom rather than his uncle Claudius. However, even in the history plays, Shakespeare discloses the personal and familial situations of those in power and of those who contest their right to hold it.

While women are typically marginal figures in the overwhelmingly patriarchal record of earlier historical epochs, Shakespeare invariably endows his female characters with extraordinary significance. In *Richard III*, for instance, the most rhetorically powerful voice in the play is that of the old widow, Queen Margaret, whose prophetic curses constitute the play's bedrock of historical truth. *Hamlet* and *Julius Caesar* also contain suicidal female characters: Hamlet's own love interest, Ophelia, drowns herself, and Portia, the wife of the conspirator Brutus, fatally swallows hot coals. Ophelia most closely resembles Desdemona from Shakespeare's later tragedy, *Othello*, in that both characters are innocent victims of the men who purport to love them. While Othello, whose mind is poisoned by the evil Iago, finally murders the loving and faithful Desdemona in a fit of virulent misogynistic rage, Hamlet – one of whose primary characteristics is not taking action – does not kill Ophelia, even though his mistreatment of her precipitates her self-destruction. Similarly, he 'will speak daggers' to his mother but determines to 'use none' (3.2.386). A further point of similarity between the two plays is that both Gertrude and Calphurnia (Caesar's wife) are the consorts of immensely powerful men whose lives unravel in spectacular ways as a consequence.

While there are, then, several connections between *Hamlet* and Shakespeare's previous plays, what is so unique about the former is that it is primarily concerned with the reasons for, and especially the consequences of, deciding not to take revenge. Laurence Olivier famously begins his film of the play with the line '*Hamlet* is the tragedy of a man who cannot make up his mind.' This pithy and ultimately inaccurate summary of the play oversimplifies Hamlet's concentrated introspection; however, it does point towards the way that *Hamlet* is more about introspection than it is about action, more about thinking rather than doing. This inertia, this entropy, is linked to the other major theme of the play: death. For death is the ultimate state of inertia. Although many critics ponder why Hamlet cannot take action, the issue is not that he lacks self-motivation. Rather, the issue is that Hamlet hesitates about committing murder, about taking away someone's life, even if that life belongs to the man who killed his father.

Historical context

At various moments in the history of *Hamlet* criticism, there have been attempts to argue that the play is almost an allegory of contemporary historical events. For example, Hamlet has been seen variously as a figure for the German Protestant reformer Martin Luther as well as a figure for King James I. However, such arguments are not only implausible, but also run counter to the necessarily open-ended nature of drama, which presses us to keep asking questions rather than to come up with pat resolutions to the problems it raises. While historical allegory is misleading, the play's historical context remains vitally important to understanding both its language and its central themes.

As we have noted, *Hamlet* was written around 1600. The preceding century had seen momentous and unprecedented change including the cataclysmic schism in Christianity – the Protestant Reformation – and the exponential growth of London as a city and, along with it, the advent of purpose-built playhouses and an ever-expanding audience for the theatre. These historical circumstances are important because by the time Shakespeare was writing *Hamlet*, some of the certainties that had structured the worldview for over a millennium and a half had been shattered, thus opening a door that had been hitherto firmly closed and locked against inquiries about religion, government, social hierarchy, the purpose of human life and the nature of the human condition. What is more, the playhouse provided a venue in which these questions might be aired. Ways of understanding the world that were before unthinkable were now possible – and some of those 'unthinkable' ideas find powerful expression in *Hamlet*.

Hamlet in criticism

There is always the danger of being overwhelmed by the amount of ink that has been spilt over *Hamlet*. So this section will give you a very brief glimpse into the myriad ways the play has been interpreted. At various key moments, this volume will guide you along some of the major trajectories of thinking about the play, but you should bear in mind that critics cannot do your thinking for you. You can agree or disagree with them, as well as use them to help shape and focus your own arguments, but it is always worth remembering that it is your argument that counts.

Hamlet is a revenge tragedy, a genre defined by action. Despite having the reputation of being the greatest of all revenge tragedies in the Western tradition, *Hamlet* is less about the act of taking revenge than it is about the act of not taking revenge. Thus, one of the most persistent questions about the play has been: Why does Hamlet delay? Answers to that question have led to a long critical tradition of understanding Hamlet as a character who is too sensitive or too much of an intellectual to act – someone who thinks too much, who is variously a neurotic dreamer or a chronic vacillator. In part because many of these (purportedly negative) qualities have been traditionally associated with women, there has been, since the nineteenth century, a tradition of women playing Hamlet, which we will address in Chapter Three. Writing in the early nineteenth century, William Hazlitt argued that when Hamlet failed to stab the praying Claudius in the back, he merely made 'an excuse for his own want of resolution' (Hazlitt, 107). So popular was this view at the time that the term 'Hamletism' became a byword for any form of dithering. In a related vein, a much more recent critic, John Kerrigan, argues that Hamlet is unable to take revenge not because he is indecisive but because he is 'stifled by remembrance' – that is, by too much mental static (Kerrigan, 186).

R. A. Foakes, however, maintains that to interpret the play as fundamentally about revenge would be mistaken, even though it is, in terms of literary categories, indeed a revenge tragedy. He argues that '[r]evenge is not the dominant concern in *Hamlet*' and that the play enables us, rather, to see revenge as repellent (Foakes, 86). Foakes acknowledges, however, that critical focus on action or inaction nonetheless responds 'in some sense to a central issue in the play, which is not the matter of revenge, but rather the control or release of instinctual drives to violence' (97). From this point of view, the only proper avengers in the play are: Pyrrhus, a figure from classical literature who avenges his father's death, narrated in the Player's speech in Act 2 scene 2; Laertes, son of the slain Polonius; and Fortinbras, son of the King of Norway (who was slain in combat by Hamlet's father) and nephew to the current monarch. For Rebecca Bushnell, too, *Hamlet* is about more than just revenge. It 'is a tragedy of knowledge as well as a revenge tragedy' (Bushnell, 71). Like Eve in the Garden of Eden, once Hamlet knows how his father died, he is compelled to wrestle with the consequences of that information and to question what he knows, as well as what he thought he knew, about every other circumstance of his being. Similarly, for the philosopher Friedrich Nietzsche, whose *The Birth of Tragedy* (1872) is one of the most important philosophical accounts of the genre in the late nineteenth century, the soul of tragedy is a figure he calls the 'Dionysiac man', an ecstatic figure named after the Greek god Dionysus who 'is similar to Hamlet: both have gazed into the true essence of things, they have acquired knowledge and they find action repulsive, for their actions can do nothing to change the eternal essence of things ... Once truth has been seen, the consciousness of it prompts man to see only what is terrible or absurd in existence wherever he looks' (qtd. in Bushnell, 70–1).

Hamlet criticism has not always been laudatory. In the twentieth century, T. S. Eliot claimed in a famous essay called 'Hamlet and His Problems' that *Hamlet* was 'most certainly an artistic failure' because Hamlet's emotions were not properly synchronized with the circumstances of the plot – that is, they lacked what Eliot called 'an objective correlative' (Eliot, 123–4). Another poet, W. H. Auden, claimed (more plausibly) that '*Hamlet* has many faults – it is full of holes both in action and motivation' (Auden, 162). Eliot and Auden went against the grain here, but while theirs were, at least in certain respects, negative assessments of *Hamlet*, they could not have been the most disconcerting to readers who were used to overlooking the play's sex and violence so that they could shelve the play away as a respectable and harmless classic. That distinction must be reserved for Ernest Jones. In a revelatory and truly original reading of the play, he applied to *Hamlet* what were at the time completely novel insights within the discipline of psychoanalysis, developed in late nineteenth-century Vienna by Sigmund Freud. Jones claimed that *Hamlet* was not really about revenge at all but rather about Hamlet's repressed desire to kill his father and have sexual relations with his mother, a phenomenon known in psychoanalysis as the Oedipus Complex, named after the title character in the ancient Greek tragedy *Oedipus Rex*, written by Sophocles c. 429 BCE. In that play, it is prophesied by the gods that Oedipus will kill his father and marry his mother and, unknowingly, he does so – only to discover at last, and to his utter horror, that the prophecy has been fulfilled. This play fascinated Freud because it was about the unknown – the 'unconscious' coming into conscious awareness. For Jones, *Hamlet* is not only a play about what the hero comes to know (his father's death), but also about what he does not and cannot know because this knowledge lies buried in his unconscious.

Perhaps unsurprisingly, every era seems to have understood *Hamlet* as its own image and likeness. The Romantic poet Samuel Taylor Coleridge, for example, envisioned Hamlet as a sensitive poetic type, much like himself. In his 'Notes on Hamlet', Coleridge wrote that the character of Hamlet 'must have some connection with the common fundamental laws of our nature', and that, '[i]n order to understand him, it is essential that we should reflect on the constitution of our own minds' (Coleridge, 145). Indeed, the focus through the years has been overwhelmingly on character criticism, especially in terms of the Prince of Denmark as a protagonist, rather than on the play as a whole. A. C. Bradley, who wrote the hugely influential *Shakespearean Tragedy* in 1904 about Shakespeare's 'great man' tragedy, focused squarely on Hamlet's tragic flaw (Bradley, 377). In the twentieth century, Hamlet's melancholy, in the face of the constraints on liberty imposed by Claudius, was understood as an all-too-relevant circumstance given the restrictions upon personal freedom imposed on those living in Eastern Communist countries. More recently, David Schalkwyk's *Hamlet's Dreams: The Robben Island Shakespeare* (2012) examined the significance that constraints on liberty in Elsinore had for Nelson Mandela and his fellow inmates of apartheid South Africa's notorious Robben Island prison. In a different key, in 'Hamlet: the Prince or the Poem?' (1942), C. S. Lewis raised the issue of whether the focus of criticism should be on character or the play itself, while Margreta de Grazia's *Hamlet Without Hamlet* (2007) reversed the critical trend of character criticism by arguing that Hamlet the character has been artificially separated from the play – especially its politics. Matters of religion have also come to the fore in Shakespeare criticism. For example, Stephen Greenblatt's *Hamlet in Purgatory* (2002) points out that the Ghost comes from Purgatory, a decidedly Catholic location despite the fact that the play was written in Protestant England at a time when Catholicism was outlawed. Similarly, for Michael Neill in his *Issues of Death* (1998), the burden of human consciousness in the play is not so much incestuous desire as it is the knowledge of human mortality, and that knowledge had been shaped by recent transformations of ideas about death in post-Reformation England.

Writing matters

Below are some strategies for beginning to read and write about *Hamlet*:

1   The best way to prepare for future writing assignments or exams on *Hamlet* is to write as you read the text: annotate, annotate, annotate. You don't have to write lengthy commentaries, but make pencil marks next to words that intrigue you or lines that sound interesting to you – even if you don't yet know what they mean. Trust yourself and your instincts. No one is looking over your shoulder, so just note your own initial responses to the text in the margins. If you have a strong reaction to a line, write it down. Importantly, write down questions that you have about the play. Answers are not what you are after right now, so focus on generating as many questions as you can.

2   Do not assume that if you don't understand something that this means you must have read the text incorrectly. As I hope you will discover in the course of this book, places where we are not sure of what is happening, or instances in which the meaning seems unclear, will often turn out to be some of the most productive avenues into developing an interpretation of the play. Later on, when you start probing these areas, they will often yield gold.

3   Remember, too, that reading takes time. The more time you put into the process of reading carefully and annotating, the better off you will be. This is not a time for speed-reading or reading plot summaries. Doing that is a bit like going to a wonderful restaurant and reading the menu without ever actually eating any of the food. No one can eat your dinner for you, so leave the plot summaries alone and dig in for yourself; otherwise, you will acquire only very superficial

knowledge of the play. Worse, in terms of your skills in relation to Shakespeare's language and your own writing, you won't be any better off than before you signed up for the course.

4 Do not expect that reading Shakespeare is ever going to be like reading your favourite mystery writer. I, for one, am very glad of that. There are innumerable treasures in *Hamlet*, and I certainly feel that my intellectual horizons expand every time I read the play. *Hamlet* is challenging – but in the best way – so don't expect easy reading and don't expect that you will not get frustrated from time to time when you have to wrangle with a dense passage. You can do it, and your reading skills and writing abilities will be immeasurably stronger as a result.

5 Write a one-sentence summary of each scene as you read. You can write more if you wish, but if you commit to one sentence you are more likely to write it consistently, and that's what counts in this stage of initial reading. You won't be able to capture everything that happens, but just the briefest outline of the main event, speech or circumstance will help jog your memory when you go back to the play. I suggest writing this at the top of the page in the edition of the play you are using. This will also give you power over the plot so that you can track the order of events in relation to the development of characters and key themes.

6 See a performance of the play. This is one of the most important things you can do early on in your engagement with the text. Bear in mind that all performances are necessarily interpretations of the play. Some are better than others; some are only loosely based on the text, while others are more concerned about fidelity to it in whatever way the director understands that. However, remember that unless your instructor specifically asks for an essay on a particular production, your work will be to analyse Shakespeare's text rather than the specific performance or movie you have watched. Nonetheless, seeing a film or stage production brings the text to life and can help you to develop your understanding of the play. I suggest starting with one of the shorter film versions of the play, such as Franco Zeffirelli's *Hamlet* (1990), or Michael Almereyda's *Hamlet* (2000).

7 You might take note of any startling changes to the text when you see the play performed on stage or screen. Are the central characters the ages you imagined them to be in your initial reading of the play? What's your sense of the age difference between Hamlet and his mother in the production you saw? Are you able to see Hamlet the character in the movie versions, or is this view obscured by the movie star personas of Mel Gibson or Ethan Hawke?

8 YouTube is a wonderful resource for watching sections of a wide range of performances (some of which are suggested at the back of this book).

CHAPTER ONE

Language in print

In this chapter we will focus on developing reading skills as the most important prerequisite to writing about *Hamlet*. First, we need to address the very practical matter of which text we are reading when we analyse and interpret the play. There are, as we shall see, a number of options here, and in the process of weighing them, we will compare two different versions of Hamlet's most famous speech. This comparison will allow us to consider what is so distinctive about Shakespeare's language. Having made our first foray into detailed analysis of a passage in the initial part of the chapter, we will then address the larger framework of Shakespeare's language constituted by the genre of revenge.

'What do you read, my lord?' (2.2.188)

Shakespeare's language is simultaneously monumental and ephemeral. In the theatre, the oral delivery of Shakespeare's poetry evaporates with the breath of the actor. Even its print transmission is unstable. We might say with *Hamlet* that the language of the play exists only 'whiles memory holds a seat / In this distracted globe' (1.5.96–7). One of the biggest problems posed by *Hamlet* is that multiple versions of the play have survived, and we do not know which one, if any of them, was the one that Shakespeare himself thought to be his full and final version. Shakespeare certainly wrote the famous line, 'To be or not to be, that is the question', but did he also write, 'To be, or not to be – ay, there's the point'? (7.115). That is the line with which Hamlet begins his most famous speech in the play in its first printing in 1603, a text which often uses language in such a way that scholars doubt that it was written by Shakespeare at all.

What we understand to be 'Shakespearean' language, then, typically derives from our experience of modern edited texts rather than from Shakespeare's plays as they were originally printed. Just as it is the surgeon's task to cut people open (albeit usually for very good reasons), it is the editor's task to modify the text, usually for very good reasons. Editors make Shakespeare's language more accessible to modern readers by correcting what they perceive to be errors and by modernizing spelling and typeface. If you look at one of the online facsimiles of *Hamlet*, you will see that early modern typefaces can be much harder to read. It is not clear, however, whether a text that has been editorially transformed remains Shakespeare's. Is it still *his* language? This question applies to any edition, not just to a text whose availability in multiple forms makes it as complex and difficult as *Hamlet*. There is, as a result, often a very substantial difference between the edited version of Shakespeare's language and the language that appeared in seventeenth-century printings of the play.

The edition of *Hamlet* to which this book refers is the Arden Shakespeare *Hamlet*, based on the Second Quarto (1604–5) text and edited by Ann Thompson and Neil Taylor. This will be our touchstone throughout. The Thompson and Taylor edition tells us upfront on the title page which early modern version of *Hamlet* it is based on (Thompson and Taylor, 139). This is important because no matter how confidently we talk about Shakespeare's language in relation to *Hamlet*, exactly what we mean by that is open to considerable dispute.

On the grounds that 'everyone knows *Hamlet*', we tend to assume that the text to which the title *Hamlet* refers is a single, solid, stable object. In fact, nothing could be farther from the truth. *Hamlet* has survived only as a printed book. There are no extant manuscript copies of any of Shakespeare's plays in his own handwriting apart from one page of a coauthored play, *Sir Thomas More*. This is how a question such as 'What is *Hamlet*?' becomes especially complicated since the play has survived in three quite different forms:

1 The First Quarto, also known as **Q1,** was printed in 1603, and there are only two surviving copies in the whole world. Sir Henry Bunbury discovered one of them in 1823 in a cupboard in his manor house. The other copy surfaced in 1856 when a Dublin bookseller bought it from an English undergraduate studying in Ireland at Trinity College. Q1 is by far the shortest of the surviving *Hamlet* texts and is approximately 2,200 lines in length.

2 The Second Quarto, also known as **Q2** (1604), is the longest of the three extant texts, coming in at almost 4,000 lines.

3 F is the version of the play printed in the First Folio (1623). F is approximately 200 lines shorter than Q2.

4 Another phantom text of the play, the lost play known as the **Ur-Hamlet** (but at the time, just called *Hamlet*), was probably not written by Shakespeare. We know that it predates the play known to us as Shakespeare's *Hamlet*, which scholars believe was written in or around 1600. The **Ur-Hamlet** is mentioned in print by Thomas Nashe in 1589 and by Thomas Lodge in 1596, as well as in the manuscript diary of the theatrical entrepreneur, Philip Henslowe, who records that it was performed in 1594.

The texts of *Hamlet*, like all other play texts of its era, are designated in terms of the size of the paper on which they were printed. 'Quarto' refers to a full folio sheet folded over into four (about the size of a modern exercise book and often with a soft cover), while 'folio' refers to a full-sized, unfolded piece of paper (roughly the size of a large, hard-bound journal). What we read on the pages of these texts was determined by the printer and by the compositors who set the typeface from either Shakespeare's handwritten copy of the play, or a 'scribal copy' – that is, a 'fair copy', a neatly handwritten version of the text made by one of the veritable army of professional writers (scribes) who flourished in Shakespeare's day. Thus, the textual choices made in terms of the text's appearance on the printed page were not necessarily those of Shakespeare himself. Once a manuscript went to the printing house, the playwright might not have had any further control over the text at all.

It is possible that Shakespeare may not have felt that a printed text was ever a final rendition of his work. Of the three versions of the play that have come down to us (respectively, **Q1, Q2**, and **F**), we simply do not know which of them – if any – was Shakespeare's last word, or his final revision of the text. More importantly, since Shakespeare worked in the dynamic environment of the theatre where scenes, characters and poetry might be changed to fit a specific performance context, alterations to the text may have been made as Shakespeare's playing company, the Lord Chamberlain's Servants (sometimes referred to as the Lord Chamberlain's Men), worked on the text in preparation for performance. Whether such changes were made and whether they were overseen or approved by Shakespeare remains a matter of scholarly debate. This does not mean, however, that Shakespeare's play texts were simply raw material for the stage. His printed playbooks, especially *Hamlet*, are often so much longer than what seems to have been the standard length of plays in Elizabethan England – or at least what the Chorus describes in *Romeo and Juliet* as 'the two hours' traffic of our stage' (Prol. 12) – that it is clear that Shakespeare understood dramatic poetry in printed form as literature also intended for reading rather than explicitly for performance. Print might record a stage in the evolution of Shakespeare's thinking about a play without being understood to petrify it – to turn it to stone, so to speak.

There is, in truth, no answer to the inevitably anachronistic question about which version of *Hamlet* is really Shakespeare's or which is the version he intended to pass on to posterity, if indeed, he gave any thought to posterity at all. Certainly, in the seventeenth century, there seems to have been less concern about establishing a single authoritative text for *Hamlet* than there was in the twentieth century, since multiple versions of Shakespeare's plays were reprinted as separate texts on several occasions. What is important here is that there is a profound paradox in that *Hamlet* – a veritable literary monument in the Western world, with all the textual certainty implied by that – is nonetheless one of the most uncertain and unstable texts in the Shakespearean canon.

Numerous theories have been proposed about the texts of *Hamlet*, among them that Q1, which was lost until its rediscovery in 1823, was a 'pirated' text – that is, a text sold to the printer without the author's knowledge or permission. The assumption in this case is that the text derived from a reconstruction of the play assembled by one of the actors who had performed in it. Another theory is that Q1 represents a version of the play taken down in inept shorthand by a member of the audience. Yet another, is that Q1 is Shakespeare's rough draft. The argument against the latter theory is, as John Jowett puts it, 'If Q1 *Hamlet* is an early draft, it represents a strange and otherwise unknown aspect of Shakespeare's writing' (Jowett, 97). Because it is understood to be a corrupt text, Q1 is often called the 'Bad Quarto'. As we shall see later in this chapter, the language of Q1 is often very far from what is traditionally considered 'Shakespearean'. Its versification is distinctly inferior and, in addition, Polonius is named Corambis, and Reynaldo is called Montano. Because Q1 is so much shorter than the other texts of *Hamlet*, some scholars argue it to have been the version of the play that was actually staged. Supporting this theory is the claim on the title page that it has been regularly performed: '[a]s it hath beene diverse times acted by his Highnesse servants in the Cittie of London: as also in the two Universities of Cambridge and Oxford, and else-where'.

Q2's frontispiece, '*THE Tragicall Historie of HAMLET, Prince of Denmarke*. By William Shakespeare', adds the following information to its title: 'Newly imprinted and enlarged to almost as much againe as it was, according to the true and perfect Coppie.' Here, the implication is that there was something decidedly *untrue* and *imperfect* about the Q1 version of the text that preceded it. Q2 was reprinted in 1611, which would seem to imply that the text was indeed a 'true and perfect' copy of Shakespeare's own manuscript. However, the 1623 Folio text, the third and last printed version of the play, published 19 years after Q2 had appeared and seven years after Shakespeare's death, differs again from Q2. We cannot dismiss such differences merely on the grounds that the Folio's version could have been a belated and posthumous printing of the play – especially as members of Shakespeare's own theatre company, John Heminges and Henry Condell, compiled it in order to acknowledge their former colleague's literary achievement. It is unlikely, then, that they would have wanted to reproduce a version of the play that was not true to his memory.

What the complicated textual history of *Hamlet* essentially points toward is that our traditional ideas about the composition and circulation of literary works are anachronistic impositions upon an Elizabethan playwright. Early modern plays were typically understood to be the property of the playing company, which, in the case of *Hamlet* was, as we have noted, the Lord Chamberlain's Servants. In the twenty-first century, a new respect for the historical fact that multiple versions of literary texts coexisted with one another has emerged out of a belief that the search for 'the real *Hamlet*' is chimerical. This is why the Arden editors, as we have noted, printed all three texts for readers to consider, even though they take Q2 to be the most reliable.

You might wonder why this matters. Can't we just rely on the scholars to sort it all out for us and settle it into one particular edition? To some degree, we can surrender ourselves to the scholarly consensus, which is by and large a text based on Q2 with supplements from the other versions where necessary or appropriate. However, we should not let editors and their respective theories make all our interpretative decisions for us. For example (and this is but one of many), only in Q1 is there a stage direction instructing Hamlet to leap into Ophelia's grave: '*Hamlet leaps in after Laertes*' (16.145); in Q2 no one leaps anywhere, and in the Folio the stage direction instructs only Laertes to jump into the grave: '*Leaps in the grave*' (5.1.247). These stage directions, or lack thereof, are important because they govern how we interpret the rivalry between Laertes and Hamlet and their respective degrees of grief over Ophelia's death. Further, while nearly all modern editions are based on Q2, they all introduce Act and scene divisions not native to the original text. So you should be aware that those breaks in the action, those segments of thought, are editorial decisions that could potentially be made very differently and thus significantly alter our understanding of the play. Most of all, we should keep in mind that our idea of a stable text is an illusion and that the edition is in part the work of the editor and not wholly the work of Shakespeare himself.

The point here is to grasp the constructed nature of any edited text – indeed, of any early modern printed text – as well as to develop a sense of the particular problems that this poses for *Hamlet*. A branch of literary studies known as 'history of the book', rather than understanding books as a means of transmitting an author's ideas to a reader – a communion of two minds facilitated by the handwritten or printed page – instead advances the argument that there is no such thing as a literary text independent of its material form because we cannot separate the language of Shakespeare's play from the physical document on which it becomes legible.

Shakespeare seems to have been thinking about this, too. In the Gravediggers' scene (5.1), for example, Hamlet is concerned with language in terms of the actual material on which it is written, namely parchment. One of the most common writing surfaces in Shakespeare's time, parchment was made from the hides of dead animals and was often used for legal documents. Having an agreement written down was understood then (much as hard copy is now) to provide tangible evidence and legal ratification that a given transaction had indeed taken place. Despite the (literally) underlying association of death with the writing surface, of which Hamlet is so keenly aware, such records were also held to constitute something permanent. Speculating that one of the skulls unearthed by the Gravedigger is that of 'a great buyer of land' (5.1.98–9) whose documents wouldn't fit in his coffin, Hamlet argues for the futility of seeking certainty and security in mortal life, when the only certainty is death. Thus, all those deeds and property titles that assured a man of his power were merely testaments to death and decay. Only fools, 'sheep and calves', seek such legal evidence:

> HAMLET   Is not parchment made of sheepskins?
> HORATIO   Ay, my lord, and of calves' skins too.
> HAMLET   They are sheep and calves which seek out
>   assurance in that.

> (5.1.107–10)

Hamlet's point is that legal evidence is already inscribed in death, even at the moment the transaction is committed to ink because it is written on part of a carcass. In other words, for Hamlet, there is no writing without death.

Shakespeare's bad language

Had Q1 been the only text of *Hamlet* that survived, the play would, undoubtedly, not be the cultural monument it has become. Several of the lines in Q1 are verbatim from the *Hamlet* we are most familiar with, especially at the beginning of the play. However, there are many other instances in which the lines sound distinctively off or 'unShakespearean'. Yet, these lines can tell us an awful lot about Shakespeare's language and why it is so powerful and effective.

For example, if we compare Q1 and Q2 at the point in the play where Horatio seeks to drink poison, and thus die in the stoic Roman fashion by committing suicide, we can see how Shakespeare's word-by-word, line-by-line choices make such an impact on the plot as a whole. First, Q1:

HORATIO
>No, I am more an antique Roman than a Dane.
>Here is some poison left.

HAMLET
>Upon my love I charge thee let it go.
>O fie, Horatio. An if thou shouldst die
>What a scandal wouldst thou leave behind?
>What tongue should tell the story of our deaths
>If not from thee? O my heart sinks, Horatio.
>Mine eyes have lost their sight, my tongue his use.
>Farewell, Horatio. Heaven receive my soul. *Dies*.

>(17.103–111)

Although some passages from Q1, as we shall see shortly, really are comically dire, this passage is not. Here, in the abbreviated and compressed action of Q1, Hamlet dies immediately. Contrast this with the edited text based on Q2, in which Hamlet does not die for another 13 lines and during which Osric arrives and Hamlet endorses Fortinbras as the new ruler of Denmark: 'he has my dying voice' (5.2.340). However, the differences between the two passages are not just those of plot, important as it may be; they are, most significantly, those of language. Consider this passage from Thompson's and Taylor's Arden edition of Q2:

HORATIO
> I am more an antique Roman than a Dane:
> Here's yet some liquor left.
HAMLET   As thou'rt a man
> Give me the cup. Let go! By heaven I'll ha't!
> O God, Horatio, what a wounded name,
> Things standing thus unknown, shall I leave behind
>   me!
> If thou didst ever hold me in thy heart
> Absent thee from felicity awhile
> And in this harsh world draw thy breath in pain
> To tell my story.

(5.2.325–33)

The language of the Q1 text is much more straightforward, conveying in blunt fashion the substance of the passage – the more literal-minded 'poison' rather than 'liquor', and 'scandal' rather than 'wounded name'. A 'wounded name' invokes the importance of maintaining the legacy of an honourable reputation by having the facts of Hamlet's death disclosed, while 'scandal' smacks of a hasty, unheroic cover-up. In Q1, Hamlet instructs his friend to put down the poisoned cup, but there is none of the struggle over it conveyed by Hamlet's injunction, 'As thou'rt a man', in Q2. Q1 has Hamlet suffer rather rapid and predictable organ failure – heart, eyes, and tongue – whereas Q2 offers a much more tender expression of Hamlet's dying love for his friend in the lyrical request that Horatio sacrifice the immediate release of death in order to exonerate him: 'Absent thee from felicity awhile' (the stress here is on *sent*, the last syllable in 'absent'). Q1 thus captures the gist of the plot here, but not the emotion that attends it.

'To be or not to be'

Q1 gives only fleeting impressions of Shakespeare's facility with language, his 'whirling words' (Q2, 1.5.132), intermixed with some oddly flat-footed forms of expression, 'To be or not to be – ay, there's the point' (Q1, 7.115) being the most famous and perhaps most egregious. This passage allows us to press upon *why*, exactly, so much of Q1's language strikes us as decidedly unpoetic, devoid of that lyrical fluency that is synonymous with Shakespeare:

> To be, or not to be – ay, there's the point.
> To die, to sleep – is that all? Ay, all.
> No, to sleep, to dream – ay, marry, there it goes,
> For in that dream of death, when we're awaked
> And borne before an everlasting judge
> From whence no passenger ever returned –
> The undiscovered country, at whose sight
> The happy smile and the accursed damned.
> But for this, the joyful hope of this,
> Who'd bear the scorns and flattery of the world –
> Scorned by the right rich, the rich cursed of the poor,
> The widow being oppressed, the orphan wronged,
> The taste of hunger, or a tyrant's reign,
> And thousand more calamities besides –
> To grunt and sweat under this weary life
> When that he may his full quietus make
> With a bare bodkin? Who would this endure,
> But for a hope of something after death,
> Which puzzles the brain and doth confound the sense –
> Which makes us rather bear those evils we have
> Than fly to others that we know not of?
> Ay, that – O, this conscience makes cowards of us all.

(Q1, 7.115–36)

In contrast with the rest of the speech, the very last line of the Q1 passage above does 'sound right' – or almost right: 'O, this conscience makes cowards of us all.' In Q2, this line reads, 'Thus conscience does make cowards –' (3.1.82), which sounds incomplete. The line we are more familiar with, 'Thus conscience does make cowards of us all' (3.1.83), is in fact from the Folio. However, there is yet another rendition of the line that we may remember as proverbial wisdom: 'Thus conscience *doth* make cowards of us all.' This version is not Shakespeare's but is an editorial and directorial invention. Perhaps the most famous use of 'doth' is in Lawrence Olivier's film, *Hamlet* (1948), which is conveniently available on YouTube: http://www.youtube.com/watch?v=ARd8aORVyoQ.

If you find yourself having difficulty understanding earlier parts of the speech from Q1, it is probably because they simply do not make sense. Some of the lines, such as Hamlet's account of death and the journey to the underworld for judgement, are jumbled and out of order, almost as if the speaker got off at several wrong exits on the way to his eternal destiny. The speech tells us that the dead never return from judgement – not, as we might logically expect, from 'The undiscovered country' of the next line. Similarly, the half-line, 'ay, marry, there it goes,' does not really carry any meaning at all: 'marry', a colloquial expression, is a mild oath used to swear 'by Mary', the Blessed Virgin, and 'there it goes' is just a rather vacant observation equivalent to the saying, 'so that's how it goes'. These empty, idiomatic expressions seem to function only to fill out the line, contrasting sharply with the pithy sentiments of every word of the speech as rendered in Q2. Now, read the more familiar version of this passage from Q2:

> To be, or not to be – that is the question;
> Whether 'tis nobler in the mind to suffer
> The slings and arrows of outrageous fortune
> Or to take arms against a sea of troubles

And by opposing end them; to die: to sleep –
No more, and by a sleep to say we end
The heartache and the thousand natural shocks
That flesh is heir to: 'tis a consummation
Devoutly to be wished – to die: to sleep –
To sleep, perchance to dream – ay, there's the rub,
For in that sleep of death what dreams may come
When we have shuffled off this mortal coil
Must give us pause: there's the respect
That makes calamity of so long life.
For who would bear the whips and scorns of time,
Th'oppressor's wrong, the proud man's contumely,
The pangs of despised love, the law's delay,
The insolence of office and the spurns
That patient merit of th'unworthy takes,
When he himself might his quietus make
With a bare bodkin. Who would fardels bear
To grunt and sweat under a weary life
But that the dread of something after death
(The undiscovered country from whose bourn
No traveller returns) puzzles the will
And makes us rather bear those ills we have
Than fly to others that we know not of.
Thus conscience does make cowards –
And thus the native hue of resolution
Is sicklied o'er with the pale cast of thought,
And enterprises of great pitch and moment
With this regard their currents turn awry
And lose the name of action.

(3.1.55–87)

Initially, we might think that the Q1 text seems jarring simply because it is unfamiliar. After all, you needn't have read *Hamlet* to know the line, 'To be, or not to be – that is the question.' There is something intrinsically risible about a misquotation – and this one is just off kilter enough to be comical. Of course, 'To be, or not to be – ay, there's the point' is not a misquotation; it's just a quotation from an alternative text. Nonetheless, the perception that it is a misquotation is perhaps what makes it sound 'off'. However, the phrase 'ay, there's the point' also jars the ear because it does not follow a regular iambic rhythm with a pattern of an unstressed syllable followed by a stressed one, and it comes right after the phrase, 'To be, or not to be', which scans with perfectly placed stresses on the second syllable of each metrical unit or foot: 'To <u>be</u>, or <u>not</u> to <u>be</u>.' However, 'To be, / or not / to be / ay, there's / the point', reads like a schizophrenic line composed by someone with a tin ear – the first part is perfect, and then the line goes strangely awry. The repetition, or **anaphora**, involved in 'To be, or not to be' creates a kind of metrical steadiness. The stress falls naturally on the 'be' of the first phrase, on the 'not' in the middle, and again on the 'be' at the end of the line. The abrupt 'ay' starts the second part of the line with a stress and the metre becomes unstable for the rest of the line. 'Ay' would work better if it followed a pause for rumination, but then the line would have too many syllables. '[P]oint' at the end of the line offers a stressed closure, which is, theoretically where the stress should be; it's just that in contrast to 'that is the question', such definitive closure is conceptually at odds with the expansive, interrogative tenor of 'To be, or not to be.'

Metrical irregularity is not necessarily a cardinal sin in poetic composition. It would be monotonous if every single line scanned 'te-<u>tum</u>, te-<u>tum</u>, te-<u>tum</u>, te-<u>tum</u>, te-<u>tum</u>' without any variation, and Shakespeare likes to play with the tune of language to very specific dramatic and lyrical effects. Indeed, the line 'To be, or not to be – that is the question' is itself an example of Shakespeare's supple and flexible use of poetic form as you will see if you sound it out. There's an extra, unstressed syllable in the '*tion*' of 'question'. This unstressed or 'feminine' ending also contains an extra syllable; there are eleven, rather than ten, syllables required by iambic pentameter. The technical term for this is a hypermetrical ending – that is, a syllable in excess of the metre. In this line, the feminine ending works to further the sense of Hamlet's inquiring frame of mind. He has not achieved resolution; he doesn't have an answer. Things are still open, up in the air, and adding that extra, unstressed beat to the line beyond the normal ten syllables conveys to us in sound this sense of not knowing – even if we are not consciously aware of it as we listen to the actor pronounce the line, or as we read it on the page. The entire passage, after all, is about the dilemma of action – if it should be taken at all and, if decided upon, how it might be effectively taken. The problem, as Shakespeare puts it in that wonderful mixed metaphor, is about whether 'to take arms against a sea of troubles'. Since weapons are not the appropriate instruments to take on the troubles of the ocean, action seems futile. Even self-destruction does not guarantee release from suffering because we do not know what awaits us after death.

Q1's version of this line, 'To be, or not to be – ay, there's the point', doesn't merely play with iambic rhythm; it abandons it altogether for an arrhythmic kind of speech that is too close to everyday utterance to count as poetry at all. This doesn't mean, of course, that you might not prefer 'ay, there's the point' just as a change from the hackneyed quotation of Q2. Conceivably, the Q1 version might cause Hamlet's existential dilemma to come upon you afresh. However, the Hamlet in Q1 is a Hamlet who can get to 'the point' and, as such, he is not the tragic hero who is the *sine qua non* of vacillation and procrastination. Interestingly, stabbing – that is, murder precisely by getting to the point, so to speak – is the main way in which Hamlet envisages taking revenge and, indeed, it is with such an instrument, the point of his rapier – 'The point envenomed' (5.2.306) at the conclusion of the play – that he finally fulfils his promise to the Ghost. In 'To be, or not to be', however, Hamlet ponders the 'bare bodkin', an unsheathed dagger or stiletto, or perhaps a long needle, with which to end his life. The Ghost takes up this image again in the closet scene. Hamlet has just confronted his mother and the spectre of his father appears before him 'to whet thy almost blunted purpose' (3.4.107). This is because in the previous scene, Hamlet took his sword out as if to kill Claudius while he was praying, only to return it to its scabbard 13 lines later. By the time the Ghost appears in Act 3 (and, notably, is seen only by Hamlet and not by his mother), Hamlet has already bungled the revenge by killing the eavesdropping Polonius. Hamlet's sword is thus potentially blunted by this misuse and needs to have its edge restored. This line is telling since the image is that of knife sharpening – as in to whet a knife by creating friction with it against a stone. In contrast, the Hamlet of Q1 who can say 'ay, there's the point', is a chap who allows no shilly-shallying about whether to do himself in. In other words, the line is inconsistent not only with the character of Hamlet that we have inherited from Q2 and F, but also with the pensive interiority, the questioning, sceptical and philosophical intelligence so apparent in the first part of the line.

Ofelia

Although it looks a little peculiar, there is nothing intrinsically wrong, comical or bizarre about the fact that the name of Hamlet's love interest is spelled in Q1 not as Ophelia but as 'Ofelia'. However, even this distinction reveals something about how Shakespeare's language works. 'Ofelia' and 'Ophelia' are homonyms – that is, they sound exactly the same; they are phonetically identical. We could make the case for some lexical sophistication in 'Ofelia' since 'filia' means 'daughter' in Latin, which would make her onomastic status, the status of her name, coincident with her designated role. So why does the spelling of 'Ofelia' look less sophisticated (albeit in a charming sort of way) than that of 'Ophelia'? It is because it looks unShakespearean. A prejudice against Ofelia might just be grounded in our familiarity with Ophelia. However, it might be more than that. Ofelia is an example of phonetic spelling – it is spelled exactly as it sounds and is thus the kind of spelling associated with limited literacy. This was the case in early modern England, even though standardized spelling had not then been instituted, just as much as it is the case today.

Is Q1 bad?

Q1 may be a 'bad' Quarto in that it is unquestionably aesthetically deficient in places when compared with Q2 and F, but is it actually *bad*? It is worth considering this question in order to become more conscious about our value judgements about literary language and about how we make evaluations about Shakespeare's aesthetic.

In Q1, the plot lines of the play are significantly altered, and there are some puzzling gaps. For instance, Q1 does not tell us how Hamlet escapes the ship taking him to certain death in England, with Horatio reporting only that he was 'set ashore' (14.26). More importantly, only in Q1 does Hamlet's mother unequivocally state that she was ignorant of the fact that her dead husband was murdered by the man she has remarried with unseemly alacrity after his death:

> But, as I have a soul, I swear by heaven
> I never knew of this most horrid murder.

(11.85–6)

In the closet scene in Q1, instead of simply attacking his mother, Hamlet persuades her to become an accomplice in his revenge against her new husband:

> And, mother, but assist me in revenge,
> And in his death your infamy shall die.

(11.95–6)

In this version, too, Gertrude agrees:

> Hamlet, I vow by that Majesty
> That knows our thoughts and looks into our hearts
> I will conceal, consent and do my best –
> What stratagem soe're thou shalt devise.

(11.97–100)

Similarly, only in Q1 is it made absolutely clear that Hamlet's mother finds out that the King has tried to have Hamlet murdered when Horatio tells her so:

> This letter I even now received of him
> Wherein he writes how he escaped the danger
> And subtle treason that the King had plotted.
> Being crossed by the contention of the winds,
> He found the packet sent to the King of England,
> Wherein he saw himself betrayed to death.

(14.2–7)

Q1 demystifies the plot and simplifies both Gertrude's character and her relationship with Hamlet – big parts of the 'mystery' of the play that have enthralled readers and audiences for centuries: What did Gertrude know, and when did she know it? In other words, Q1 explains away much of the intrigue that makes *Hamlet Hamlet*.

Despite these problems, however, Q1 has its merits. Because it is so much shorter, Q1 allows for some alacrity, pace and rhythm in performance. Even those who have not witnessed a performance based on the First Quarto in the theatre might find themselves leaning towards it after watching Kenneth Branagh's four-hour-long film version of the play, or even a marathon five-hour performance of a so-called 'full-text' *Hamlet* in the theatre. While 'the two hours' traffic of our stage' (Prol. 12) referred to by the Chorus at the opening of *Romeo and Juliet* gives us the impression that attention spans of Elizabethan audiences were rather like our own, a four- or five-hour viewing of *Hamlet*, especially given the requirements of modern audiences to sit still in the dark (you could have at least moved around in the pit in Shakespeare's day), feels like an endurance test. On the other hand, the play's length increases the emphasis on the hero's failure to avenge his father's death and allows time for other revenge plots to multiply, such as those of Pyrrhus, Laertes, and Fortinbras. Hamlet's revenge, when it finally occurs at the end of three or four hours, seems hopelessly belated. From this point of view, the length is dramaturgically effective and permits a space for thought, so that we can 'consider curiously' (5.1.195) along with Hamlet.

Genre

The remainder of this chapter will address the question of genre – that is to say, the literary category that *Hamlet* falls into, namely that of revenge tragedy. While there is an element of revenge in many of Shakespeare's histories and tragedies, and even, as we shall see, in some of the comedies, his two full-fledged revenge plays are *Hamlet* and the early Roman history play, *Titus Andronicus*. The latter play features swift payback for the Romans' murder of the son of Tamora, Queen of the Goths. Thereafter, bloody deed follows upon bloody deed in a chain of retributive violence, whose culminating carnage includes, along with a theatrically satisfying round of stabbings, two rapists baked in a pie and fed to their own mother. There is a lot less gore in *Hamlet* but, like *Titus Andronicus*, the plot is propelled by the idea that an initial wrong must be avenged. However, if revenge is the mechanism that typically propels tragedy along its predestined course, Hamlet's hesitation in fulfilling his promise to the Ghost to avenge his father's death represents a deviation from revenge tragedy's more orthodox structure, an innovation in the genre that also problematizes the decorum of revenge tragedy itself. While the idea that moral scruples might impede speedy retribution became less unusual in revenge tragedies of the early seventeenth century (largely because of the influence of *Hamlet*), in *Hamlet* this delay is foregrounded to the point where more of the play is about not taking vengeance than about taking it. That is, the play manipulates and reverses some of the most conventional elements of revenge tragedy. Indeed, *Hamlet* is, in many ways, a revenge play manqué, or an 'unrevenge' play, despite sharing so many common characteristics of revenge tragedy, such as the Ghost, the melancholic hero, suicide, and the theme of madness. What fills that lacuna in terms of action is Hamlet's astonishing capacity for introspection – his dilation on the self, his capacity to articulate and enlarge on his dilemma. This amplification of Hamlet's thoughts and feelings is a dramatic strategy that allows Shakespeare to make the play at least as much about Hamlet's reaction to his predicament as it is about revenge.

'Poem unlimited'?

Genre is also a significant topic of conversation when the players who will later perform the play-within-the-play arrive in Elsinore. Polonius describes their astonishing range, and in doing so delineates not only the central division in theatrical genres between tragedy and comedy, but also the hodgepodge of possible genre combinations in between:

> The best actors in the world, either for
> tragedy, comedy, history, pastoral, pastoral-comical,
> historical-pastoral, scene individable or poem
> unlimited. Seneca cannot be too heavy nor Plautus too
> light for the law of writ and the liberty.

> (2.2.333–8)

In its purest form, comedy, represented in this instance by Plautus, the Roman comic playwright, is 'light' not because it is vacuous or superficial, but because of the emotional release afforded by laughter. Tragedy, represented here by Seneca, the Roman precursor of Elizabethan revenge drama, is heavy with the pain and suffering generated by violence. History is not just an account of the past but implies something akin to our modern notion of biography. Pastoral is a genre derived from the Greek poet, Theocritus, whose *Idylls* are ostensibly the songs of herdsmen set in an idealized rural landscape. These literary forms sit between the two poles of the genre spectrum, as do the less orthodox combinations of genre categories, 'pastoral-comical, historical-pastoral'. By way of suggesting the infinite capacities of the actors who have arrived in Elsinore – they can play anything – Polonius even adds a couple of nonsense options: 'scene individable or poem unlimited'.

While Polonius' all-inclusive list of literary categories accurately describes a wide range of theatrical genres deployed by playwrights at the end of the sixteenth century, this does not mean that in Elizabethan England dramatic poetry was literally 'unlimited'. This was not a world that possessed the concept of 'free speech', at least not in our modern sense. Thomas Wilson's popular book, *The Art of Rhetoric* (1553) did include the category, 'freeness of speech' (Wilson, 107v), but this referred to ideas derived from ancient Greek tenets of rhetoric about avoiding flattery when speaking to social superiors and about the importance of frank exchange and the avoidance of duplicity among social equals. These codes of conduct were appropriate only to an elite minority of free male citizens (Colclough, 40). Had it been conceived of at all in Shakespeare's day (and, by and large, it wasn't), our democratic understanding of free speech would have been thought dangerously anathema to the good of civil society. Everything Shakespeare wrote was subject to censorship by the Revels Office, which controlled theatrical performances, and by the Stationers' Company, the licensing authority for everything printed in England. On a social and, indeed, geographical level, too, there were restrictions on theatrical performances, and it is to these strict regulations that Polonius' comment about 'the law of writ' refers. Within the City of London, plays could be performed only in areas known as 'liberties'; otherwise, like the Globe which stood on the south side of the River Thames, playhouses had to be situated outside the city walls. In the play, Hamlet is keenly aware of the limitations on what he can say and that speech, in all its forms, can be politically dangerous: 'I must hold my tongue' (1.2.159). Beyond legal restrictions and political pressure, however, there were more specific literary protocols that helped shape the language of *Hamlet*. These are precisely those of genre. Just as modern audiences approach soap operas with different expectations from those of horror films, genre categories mattered in Shakespeare's time because they constituted a broad framework through which specific types of literary language were understood.

The quasi-technical rules for tragedy, or tragic decorum, derived from ancient Greek theatre, and failure to observe them sometimes excited censure. Indeed, in his immensely influential *The Defence of Poesy* (1595), Philip Sidney condemns the intermingling of genres as 'nothing but scurrility unworthy of chaste ears', since they were 'neither right tragedies nor right comedies' (Alexander, 46–7). *Hamlet* itself, however, stands in violation of discrete genre classifications from its very title page as being neither history nor tragedy but a mingle-mangle of the two: *THE Tragicall Historie of HAMLET, Prince of Denmarke* (only in the Folio does the title read simply as *The Tragedie of Hamlet, Prince of Denmark*). Regardless of Polonius' faults as a 'wretched, rash, intruding fool' (3.4.29), his excitement about plays and about the myriad genre possibilities they afford is infectious. The genre to which *Hamlet* comes closest in Polonius' catalogue is, of course, that of tragedy, and particularly that of revenge tragedy, so closely associated with Seneca.

Tragedy

Genre categories and the characteristics proper to tragedy were first outlined in Aristotle's *Poetics* (c. 335 BCE). Aristotle defined tragedy as the dramatic imitation of action in a situation that is clearly of some considerable human significance – in other words, the 'Big Picture' of life and its meaning. Thus, Aristotle argued that 'tragedy is mimesis not of persons but of action and life; and happiness and unhappiness consist in action' (Aristotle, 51). By 'action' Aristotle meant situation or predicament, and for him, the action is characterized by the intense emotions of pity and fear, and moves through a process of purification or catharsis. Crucially, for our purposes this drama is delivered 'in language embellished by distinct forms in its sections' (Aristotle, 47). Aristotle used the word 'embellished' for 'language with rhythm and melody', while 'distinct forms in its sections' referred to 'the fact that some parts are conveyed through metrical speech alone, others through song' (Aristotle, 48). Interestingly, when Thomas Nashe mentioned the *Ur-Hamlet* (the lost play that predates Shakespeare's *Hamlet*) in his preface to Robert Greene's *Menaphon* (1589), he called it 'English Seneca', and focused not on matters of plot device and action but on 'good sentences' and 'tragical speeches' (Nashe was something of a close reader) (Nashe, 474). Thus the rules, or 'decorum', of tragedy are not all about the plot. On the contrary, Aristotle's list of characteristics describing the formal qualities of tragedy included 'verbal expression' and 'thought' or intellectual substance alongside plot and character (Aristotle, 53).

Revenge tragedy

Hamlet's delay in taking action constitutes a major deviation from the traditional trajectory of the revenge tragedy genre. Revenge drama revolves around payback murders, and it is one of the oldest dramatic forms in Western literature. Perennially popular, it is still the stuff of action movies. The wonderful thing about revenge, from a dramaturgical point of view, is that it provides a motor for the plot: once the keys are in the ignition, so to speak, with ever-accelerating momentum, the multiple-collision effect of retribution culminates in a heap of dead bodies. The action of the play is marked by a series of atrocities that constitute the avenger's path throughout the play until he himself is also murdered or commits suicide. In combination with numerous Italian influences, particularly Machiavellianism (Claudius is an example of the Machiavellian villain), works such as Thomas Kyd's *The Spanish Tragedy* (c. 1587) and Thomas Newton's *Seneca his Ten Tragedies, Translated into English* (1581) began to form a kind of template for English revenge tragedy. These influences created the conventions of the genre – that is, they helped constitute the shape and framework of most revenge tragedies circulating around the time that Shakespeare was writing *Hamlet*.

The most important precursor to *Hamlet* in English drama was Thomas Kyd's *The Spanish Tragedy*. The plot is almost a mirror image of *Hamlet*'s because it is about the belated vengeance of Hieronimo for the murder of his son, Horatio. The play begins with the ghost of Don Andrea, who has been slain in battle by Balthazar. Don Andrea is accompanied by Revenge, who is an actual character in the play. As in the Senecan tradition, Don Andrea and Revenge serve as a chorus between acts. Revenge promises Don Andrea that he will see his mistress, Bel-imperia, avenge his death, and they then sit and watch as events in the mortal realm unfold. In the course of those events, Horatio's mother goes mad and kills herself, while Hieronimo also seems to suffer from 'brainsick lunacy' (4.4.118). Like Hamlet, Hieronimo does not 'sweep' to revenge, but cautiously awaits more evidence. Finally, Hieronimo tells his enemies (shades of Polonius) that while he was at the University of Toledo, he composed a tragedy, and he persuades them to act in it. This play-within-the-play turns out to be a 'snuff' drama: Bel-imperia kills Balthazar and then kills herself, and Hieronimo kills the evil Lorenzo. Hieronimo reveals that the deaths have not been acting but real; he bites out his tongue and stabs himself. The ghost, suicide, the madness both real and feigned, the play-within-the-play and especially Hieronimo's delay in executing the revenge all offer parallels with *Hamlet*. What is decidedly different is the stiffer, more formal diction of Kyd's tragedy, which took Senecan tragedy as its rhetorical model.

Right revenge

Even more than other types of tragedy, revenge tragedy is not just different from comedy but diametrically opposed to it. In comedy, the reigning emotional tenor is that of reconciliation. The focus is on mending social ties and the celebration of community. Revenge, in contrast, is built upon the deliberate and wilful destruction of social bonds. A revenge plot gains momentum, barrelling on, hell-bent upon the untimely death of everyone in its path, including the protagonist.

However, revenge is not exclusive to tragedy. It does occasionally appear in comedy, although in comedies the injured party takes the task of vengeance upon himself entirely of his own volition. In Shakespeare's festive comedy, *Twelfth Night*, for example, Malvolio, who has been ridiculed, humiliated and imprisoned, at length declares, 'I'll be revenged on the whole pack of you' (5.1.371). This is, nonetheless, a disconcerting moment that shadows the otherwise happy ending of the play. For Malvolio, it's not all over (which, of course, is one of the features of revenge); there's always payback, and there remains an uneasy sense of unfinished business at the close of *Twelfth Night*. For all that, there is no suspicion that the other characters in the play should expect to be murdered in their beds, or poisoned in their orchards at the hands of Malvolio. Thus, the play is still contained within the boundaries of its genre. Revenge is also a significant feature of *The Merry Wives of Windsor*, which, like *Hamlet*, concerns itself with the potential threat of adultery. However, the forms of vengeance involved in *Merry Wives* are wholly comic and are rituals of social shaming rather than murder.

Unusually for a comedy, in *Much Ado About Nothing*, one of Shakespeare's liveliest female characters, Beatrice, enjoins Benedick, who has only moments before declared his love for her, to avenge the slander done to her cousin. Hero has been falsely and publicly accused by her fiancé, Claudio, of being a 'wanton':

> BENEDICK   … I
>   protest I love thee.
> BEATRICE   Why then, God forgive me.
> BENEDICK   What offence, sweet Beatrice?
> BEATRICE   You have stayed me in a happy hour; I was
>   about to protest I loved you.
> BENEDICK   And do it, with all thy heart.
> BEATRICE   I love you with so much of my heart that
>   none is left to protest.
> BENEDICK   Come, bid me do anything for thee.
> BEATRICE   Kill Claudio.
>
>   (4.1.278–88)

There are several ways in which this exchange makes a compelling parallel to the revenge scenario in *Hamlet*. To begin with, there is the onomastic coincidence between Claudius, the 'bloody, bawdy villain' (2.2.515) in *Hamlet*, and Claudio. Benedick also shares Hamlet's doubt about the legitimacy of the order to take revenge. This is not because he questions whether Beatrice is good or evil, as Hamlet does the Ghost, but because he is unsure of Hero's innocence. Benedick's response to Beatrice's injunction, 'Kill Claudio', is unequivocally negative: 'Ha, not for the wide world' (4.1.89). Of course, Benedick is being commanded to revenge by a flesh-and-blood mortal, not by a ghost, and it is, perhaps, easier to dialogue with the living than with the dead. Only when Beatrice convinces Benedick that Claudio's public accusation of unchastity against Hero is wholly unfounded does Benedick agree to challenge Claudio to a duel.

While Beatrice's command is powerfully forthright, the Ghost's injunction to revenge is as unnatural as the 'foul and most unnatural murder' (1.5.25) he wishes Hamlet to avenge on his behalf. Both are instances of private revenge or vendetta, what Sir Francis Bacon, in his essay 'Of Revenge' (1625) called 'a kind of wild Justice' (Bacon, 9). Revenge was then, as now, against the law. Despite this legal prohibition, however, there remained considerable sympathy for revenge, and the most justifiable form of vengeance was felt to be that in which there was no possibility of legal resolution. Bacon writes, 'The most tolerable sort of *Revenge*, is for those wrongs which there is no Law to remedy' (Bacon, 10). As a slandered woman accused by a nobleman and a prince, there is no legal recourse for Hero, and since in *Hamlet*, Claudius, the murderer, is king, these are both instances in which revenge promises the only avenue to justice.

Tragic precedent

Revenge literature is at least 3,000 years old, and drama in particular has been the supreme vehicle of the genre. Some of the West's oldest tragedies, such as those of ancient Greece, concern vengeance required of a son by a father. In Euripides' *Orestes*, written in fifth century BCE Athens, for example, the hero is tasked with destroying his mother who has murdered his father. Shakespeare is thus writing within a very well-established genre, and he pays homage to precursors like *The Spanish Tragedy* just in the same way as movie directors today pay homage to other films.

Hamlet is revenge with a major twist in that, instead of burning to achieve retribution like Laertes, the hero is a reluctant avenger – hesitant, ponderous and plagued by suicidal thoughts. But the twist is only effective because Shakespeare and his audience are so thoroughly immersed in the conventions of revenge tragedy. Indeed, arguably what makes Hamlet such an astonishing character is that he does not seem to belong to the genre. We may be able to recognize more readily how *Hamlet* deviated from the conventions of revenge drama if, instead of looking only at the origins of revenge tragedy in the works of the classical Greek playwrights Euripides, Sophocles and Aeschylus – and especially in the works of the Roman dramatist, Seneca –, we look *forward* to modern examples of the revenge genre. Particularly conspicuous examples of modern alterations of the genre are those where women take revenge for sexual violation either on their own behalf or on behalf of a female relative. Examples of this phenomenon, whose first emergence coincided with the women's movement of the 1970s, include the *Kill Bill* movies (2003 and 2004) directed by Quentin Tarantino, where a woman takes spectacularly gory revenge on the men who have raped her. As Carol J. Clover points out, '[I]n the spate of rape-revenge films … rape becomes a problem for women themselves to solve' (Clover, 138). Classic examples include *I Spit on Your Grave* (1978), *Act of Vengeance* (1974), *The Accused* (1988) and more recently, *Hard Candy* (2005), where a 14-year-old girl is the surprising avenger. Just as Hamlet as the indecisive hero constitutes a departure from the bloodthirsty, enraged avenger who acts without much in the way of thought at all, let alone serious contemplation, the female rape victim as avenger deviates from the tradition, both cultural and cinematic, whereby a male relative takes revenge for a woman's dishonour. An example of this convention is Ingmar Bergman's movie, *The Virgin Spring* (1960), which treats a father's gruesome retribution for the rape of his virgin daughter who was assaulted on her way to church. In *Last House on the Left* (1972), both parents take revenge on behalf of their raped and murdered daughter, but the mother offers to fellate the rapist and then, in a startling instance of female retribution, bites off his penis (Clover, 137). Like *Hamlet*, these films represent significant changes in the form and medium of revenge and press us, just as Shakespeare's play does, to consider more carefully the nature of the crime that is being punished and to ask questions about who, if anyone, has the right to revenge, and to whom revenge belongs. Centuries of commentary have labelled Hamlet as a 'failed' avenger, as we have already seen for example, in Laurence Olivier's prefatory summation of the play as 'the tragedy of a man who cannot make up his mind' in the film, *Hamlet* (1948). However, considering the play in the context of these modern revenge films demonstrates how such commentary misses the play's radical interrogation of unthinking violence. Shakespeare's goal does not seem to be that of having Hamlet become Pyrrhus, plastered 'head to foot' '[w]ith the blood of fathers, mothers, daughters, sons' (2.2.394; 396). Instead, *Hamlet* is profoundly critical of this 'ideal' of revenge.

The pre-Christian, classical tradition condoned revenge. The Greek goddess, Nemesis, the deity of remorseless retributive justice is referred to in *The Spanish Tragedy* as 'wrathful Nemesis, that wicked power' (1.4.16). Unlike the Christian deity, she shows no mercy; Nemesis executes, unflinchingly and unwaveringly, divine justice. Christianity, of course, forbade revenge. The Old Testament prohibition against revenge was reiterated by St. Paul: 'Dearly beloved, avenge not yourselves, but give place unto wrath: for it is written, Vengeance is mine: I will repay, saith the Lord' (Romans 12.19). However, biblical precepts about revenge were contradictory. In Deuteronomy (32.35), God claims the right to vengeance, whereas instructions were given earlier in that same book of the Bible to deliver murderers to the relatives of their victims to be killed. In the Book of Numbers, revenge is likewise condoned: 'The revenger of blood [a male relative] himself shall slay the murderer: when he meeteth him, he shall slay him (Numbers 35.19). Even St. Paul's scriptural evidence against revenge implies that God is himself an avenger because vengeance belongs to him. Unlike some of the Italian city-states, where revenge was legal under certain circumstances, in early modern England all acts of private revenge were officially condemned. The state sought to maintain the prerogative to punish homicide as well as other crimes, but the widespread and repeated legal and ecclesiastical condemnation of revenge argued that violations of the prohibition were many. Settling scores by duelling, in particular (which is, of course, the focus of *Hamlet*'s tragic denouement), increasingly became a problem for authorities in Jacobean England. Despite the oft-iterated religious prohibition against revenge in early modern England, it remained then (and, alas, now) a completely plausible motivation and rationale for murder. The jurist and philosopher Francis Bacon wrote of the legal and religious prohibitions against vengeance:

> *Revenge* is a kind of wild Justice; which the more Man's Nature runs to, the more ought Law to weed it out. For as the first wrong, it doth but offend the Law, but the Revenge of that wrong putteth the Law out of Office. Certainly in taking *Revenge*, a Man is but even with his Enemy; but in passing it over he is superior: for it is a Princes part to pardon. And Solomon, I am sure, saith, *It is the Glory of a Man to pass by an offence* (Bacon, 10–11).

Bacon recognizes that the impulse toward revenge is natural, an all-too-human response to wrongdoing. It is 'wild' – that is, potentially both spontaneous (rather than premeditated) and uncivilized. However, while the initial crime clearly contravenes the legal statute against homicide or other criminal acts, the payback crime usurps the place of judge and jury in deciding on guilt and punishment. Bacon's final biblical reference suggests that forgiveness is much less common than getting even.

Interestingly, while Hamlet expresses specifically religious scruples about committing suicide, wishing 'that the Everlasting had not fixed / His canon 'gainst self-slaughter. O God, God' (1.2.131–2), he expresses none about revenge. Perhaps this is because there was no ethical dilemma about revenge in the historical account written by Saxo Grammaticus. There, in the pre-Christian world of King Feng (the Claudius figure), Amleth (the Hamlet figure) is understood to have a filial *obligation* to avenge his father's death. Hamlet, however, does have a strong, decidedly Christian sense that he is the instrument of providential justice used by God to right the wrongs that have been committed in the state of Denmark: 'O cursed spite / That ever I was born to set it right!' (1.5.186–7). Providentialism was a characteristically Protestant idea that bad things happened to the wicked as God's punishment and was in some ways a Christian renovation on the classical idea of fate. Such competing ideas about vengeance contained within the play make *Hamlet* an intensely self-reflexive revenge tragedy that presses audiences and readers to reconsider their presumptions about revenge in general and about whether retributive violence can ever constitute justice.

Reflections on revenge

Hamlet contains not only a number of distinct and contra-dictory ideological and ethical ideas about revenge, but also different images of the avenger, including the ultimately victo-rious Fortinbras who brings about the plot's final resolution. Laertes is the alternate avenger with whom the audience spends the most time, and he explicitly defies the Christian prohibition against revenge when he declares he will 'dare damnation' (4.5.132) in order to accomplish it. In The *Wheel of Fire* (1930), the twentieth-century critic Wilson Knight found Laertes a breath of fresh air after Hamlet's protracted vacillation (Knight, 40). However, he is also rash and almost a demonic mirror of Hamlet as an avenging son. In terms of the play's structure, Laertes certainly provides the kind of clear intent to act that the audience expects from the revenge genre, but his character functions as a foil to Hamlet as well as a means of highlighting the very legitimate concerns Hamlet voices about vengeance. Laertes has no second thoughts: 'Let come what comes, only I'll be revenged / Most throughly for my father' (4.5.134–5). Like a Senecan avenger, the furious Laertes intends to pay back with interest the wrongs done to his family. When he sees his sister driven to insanity he swears, 'By heaven, thy madness shall be paid with weight / Till our scale turn the beam' (4.5.155–6). The image here is of two scales hanging by a bar, with the 'beam' tilting towards the heavier weight. Laertes' commitment to revenge is premeditated, calculated and exact, as well as a direct contradiction of one of the most ancient principles of retaliation: 'eye for eye, tooth for tooth'. Found in the ancient Babylonian Code of Hammurabi and later in Mosaic Law (Lev. 24.20, Exod. 21.24 and Deut. 19.21), this precept, known in Latin as *lex talionis*, argues for the acceptability of retaliation in exact proportion (and, crucially, no more) – that is, precisely even with the original offence.

In *Hamlet*, the classical precursor for such enraged single-mindedness, as well as the desire for 'overkill' (getting more than even), is the figure of Pyrrhus, the son of the Greek warrior Achilles, who hides in the Trojan horse in order to avenge his father's death on Priam, the aged King of Troy. This story, from Book II of Virgil's *Aeneid* (c. 29–19 BCE), is recounted by one of the Players and has significant parallels to Hamlet's revenge. First, Pyrrhus misses his target (as Hamlet does when he kills Polonius) 'in rage strikes wide' (2.2.410), and then there is an intriguing moment when Pyrrhus' sword is suspended in mid air in a kind of freeze-frame, as if time stops, just before he takes his revenge:

> *a hideous crash*
> *Takes prisoner Pyrrhus' ear. For lo, his sword*
> *Which was declining on the milky head*
> *Of reverend Priam seemed i'th' air to stick.*

So as a painted tyrant Pyrrhus stood
Like a neutral to his will and matter,
Did nothing.
But as we often see against some storm
A silence in the heavens, the rack stand still,
The bold winds speechless and the orb below
As hush as death, anon the dreadful thunder
Doth rend the region, so after Pyrrhus' pause
A roused vengeance sets him new a-work
And never did the Cyclops' hammers fall
On Mars's armour, forged for proof eterne,
With less remorse than Pyrrhus' bleeding sword
Now falls on Priam.

(2.2.414–30)

These opponents are *'unequal matched'* (2.2.409); Priam is frail, old, *'reverend'*, white-haired (or *'milky'*) and has lost his weapon. This passage thus recounts the execution of remorseless vengeance on a defenceless old man. The relentless brutality of the assault, however, also contains a moment of delay, an interval between the intention to take revenge and the achievement of it: *'Pyrrhus' pause.'* He hesitates for a moment, as still as a figure in a painting, upon hearing the crash of the burning city. For that split second, like the temporary stillness in the eye of a storm, he is *'[l]ike a neutral'* – that is, like someone devoid of will and purpose. It is a momentary impotence.

'[M]atter', in the line *'Like a neutral to his will and matter'*, is a word the audience heard earlier when Polonius asked Hamlet what 'matter' he was reading (2.2.190). Polonius meant subject matter, but Hamlet deliberately took him to mean quarrel, the kind of altercation that might, in Shakespeare's time, be the reason for a duel in order to satisfy (quite illegally) the perceived necessity for retribution in order to save one's honour. In this passage, however, *'will and matter'* means desire and duty. The following short line, *'Did nothing*' enacts the dramatic pause here in Pyrrhus' onslaught as the missing syllables of the iambic line are filled out with silence. Importantly, however, whereas Hamlet's hesitation about killing Claudius is characterized by deep thought, no meditation – no thought process of any kind – is registered in the interval during which Pyrrhus' action is suspended. (Avengers are not generally thoughtful people.)

Pyrrhus is capable of sense perception (he hears the crash) but not of reflection, which might cause him to desist from battering and hacking an old man to pieces. After the pause, the onslaught continues more ferociously than ever. Like the mythical smithies, the Cyclops, who work for the blacksmith deity, Vulcan, to forge invincible armour for Mars, the god of war, Pyrrhus hammers on his adversary without conscience or remorse. That Pyrrhus is also like a painting – both motionless and painted in blood – also draws our attention to the ways in which revenge is the subject matter for art, including *Hamlet* itself. When the actors play *The Murder of Gonzago*, even though revenge is not a component of what they perform, Hamlet calls out a paraphrased version of lines from an actual play from the period, *The True Tragedy of Richard III* (c. 1591): 'the croaking raven doth bellow for revenge' (3.2.247). Painting and plays are cultural pauses for reflection on the violent processes of revenge.

'Now to my word' (1.5.110)

'Revenge' is both the genre that structures *Hamlet* and one of the most important words in the play. Further, there is a sense that Hamlet's absorption in language ('my word') is a key obstacle that lies between him and the violent action he has sworn to undertake. When Claudius urges Laertes to avenge his father's death, he does so by opposing deeds and words:

KING

> What would you undertake
> To show yourself in deed your father's son
> More than in words?

LAERTES To cut his throat i'th' church.

KING

> No place indeed should murder sanctuarize.

> (4.7.122–5)

The church was traditionally a place of refuge where one could not be arrested, but revenge has no restrictions for a traditional avenger like Laertes. It is this that makes Laertes' revenge illicit despite the arguably technical legality of being instructed to undertake it by the king. As Claudius puts it in an exchange that is almost a reprisal of the Ghost's interview with Hamlet, 'Revenge should have no bounds' (4.7.126). Even in early modern England, the king was not above the law. Claudius's focus in these lines is upon the antithesis between 'words' and 'deed', and the implication is that 'words' – that perhaps even language itself – could prove to be an impediment to an ireful vengeance that is so focused on its accomplishment that it leaves no room for the mental processes of language, for spoken or unspoken words.

The word 'revenge' itself first appears in *Hamlet* at the beginning of Hamlet's interview with the Ghost in Act 1, scene 5.

HAMLET Alas, poor ghost.

GHOST

> Pity me not, but lend thy serious hearing
> To what I shall unfold.

HAMLET Speak, I am bound to hear.

GHOST

> So art thou to revenge when thou shalt hear.

HAMLET
  What?

> (1.5.4–8)

The word is repeated as the Ghost delivers his mission to Hamlet:

GHOST
    If thou didst ever thy dear father love –
HAMLET
    O God!
GHOST
    – Revenge his foul and most unnatural murder!

                                    (1.5.23–5)

In revenge tragedies such as Shakespeare's earlier *Titus Andronicus*, once the grim assignment has been arrived upon, the protagonist goes out and takes revenge as instructed, setting off a chain of bloody murder and mayhem. *Hamlet*, of course, deviates from this formula, so it is important that his delay remain compelling to the audience who might otherwise become bored while waiting for the other shoe to drop.

The interrogative, 'What?' after Hamlet first hears the word 'revenge' indicates the incomprehension and disbelief with which he receives the command to revenge and is one of a series of inquiries into things both terrestrial (e.g. his mother's sexuality) and supernatural (what happens after death) – things which cannot fully be known or revealed. Further, Hamlet's brief ejaculations, those short lines that register his shock – 'What?' and 'O God!' – are followed by complete iambic lines. Thus they offer a space, a pause, for the audience to take in the key word of the previous line: 'Revenge.'

Hamlet's response to the Ghost's directive is that he needs to know more:

    Haste me to know't that I with wings as swift
    As meditation or the thoughts of love
    May sweep to my revenge.

                                    (1.5.29–31)

The 'wings as swift' sweeping are sure signs of action. But is 'meditation' swift? While the speed of thought itself is indeed something to be reckoned with, meditation implies a ponderousness that contradicts the speedy retribution to which Hamlet gives his provisional promise – a promise contingent upon his being fully informed about the circumstances of the murder. '[T]houghts of love' also seem somewhat out of place in this line. Hamlet indeed loved his father, but these particular thoughts take us into the territory of leisurely romantic daydreaming, something that belongs to a different literary genre altogether and which seems entirely at odds with the information that has just been delivered to him:

> I could a tale unfold whose lightest word
> Would harrow up thy soul, freeze thy young blood
>
> (1.5.15–16)

There are no light words in revenge tragedy. The Ghost's description of his torments would have immediately dire and specifically somatic effects on Hamlet. Similarly, Hamlet's oath to take revenge, his 'word', is freighted with the most terrifying consequences. That weight is the burden of the past upon the present and of the dead upon the living.

The idea of the dead returning in tragedy is an ancient one. Indeed, the earliest complete tragedy that survives, Aeschylus's *The Persians* (472 BCE), is a play about divine retribution for hubris in which the ghost of a king returns from the dead to condemn his son for the mismanagement of his empire. The dead king has already been deified, so there is no doubt about the veracity of his pronouncements. Scholars do not believe that this play was in circulation in Shakespeare's England. Nonetheless, there is a cultural continuity in the development of revenge tragedy as a genre that makes the similarities of the situation almost uncanny.

Revenge and memory

Mimnēskō, the Greek word for remember, has, historically, also been part of the revenge tradition because the avenger must recall the injury done to the original victim. In Aeschylus' *Libation Bearers*, part of the *Oresteia* trilogy, (performed 458 BCE), Orestes and his sister Electra remind themselves of the wrongs done to their father:

ORESTES
        Remember the bath – they stripped away your life
            my father.
ELECTRA
        Remember the all-embracing net – they made it
            first for you

                                                    (*l.* 478–9)

When the Ghost departs by saying, 'Adieu, adieu, adieu, remember me' (1.5.91), Hamlet declares his promise but, crucially, that promise is not, in fact, to avenge his father's death, but to remember him:

                    Now to my word.
    It is 'Adieu, adieu, remember me.'
    I have sworn't.

                                                    (1.5.110–12)

The oath of remembrance is not to any particular action, but perhaps to some rite or ritual of memory which, as a number of critics have suggested, is reminiscent of the pre-Reformation practice of praying for the dead and especially of offering Masses for the release of souls believed to be in Purgatory. Remembrance, however, is also an internal, mental rehearsal of the departed person's life, a process of thinking about the deceased, which implies, in a sense, that Hamlet is promising no action of any kind – only to think more about his dead father. That memory is key to *Hamlet* is cued numerous times throughout the play, such as Hamlet's reference to 'th'arithmetic of memory' (5.2.100), Ophelia's plangent 'There's rosemary: that's for remembrance' (4.5.169), and Fortinbras' claim to 'some rights of memory in this kingdom' (5.2.373).

As the Player King remarks in the play-within-the-play: '*Purpose* [intention] *is but the slave to memory*' (3.2.182). Claudius, too, is aware of this when he spurs Laertes to revenge, reminding him that 'Time qualifies the spark and fire' (4.7.111) required for revenge:

> That we would do
> We should do when we would, for this 'would' changes
> And hath abatements and delays.

> (4.7.116–18)

Hamlet promises the Ghost that he will remember nothing else. In a sense, that is all he does – he remembers – and his ruminations result in delay and, at a vital moment when Claudius is vulnerable, presumably praying, with his back to Hamlet, he misses his opportunity with the carefully crafted theological rationale that Claudius might go to heaven if killed while praying. Celestial bliss, of course, is more than his father's murderer deserves. In the wake of this hesitation, the Ghost is required to appear again to spur on Hamlet's 'dull revenge' (4.4.32).

The nature of revenge, of course, is that it's not something you need to be reminded of. Typically, those who have been injured relish the rehearsal of their grievances. Avengers are bloody-minded and bent on their goal: the destruction of whomever has done them wrong. The Ghost seems to have some intimation that Hamlet is not like this, given his final words during his first appearance to his son: 'remember me' (1.5.91). Much has been made of the theological significance of this reminder because it echoes the Eucharistic rite of the recently proscribed Catholic Mass (it was against the law to practise Roman Catholicism in Shakespeare's England). However, there is also a sense that Hamlet is forgetful. When he declares that all other 'fond records' (1.5.99), or memories, will be obliterated save the Ghost's injunction, the image that he uses is that of a table book, or a notebook. The avenger typically does not have time to consult notebooks, physical or metaphorical. Hamlet, however, consults both, and after some 15 lines of declaring that he cannot forget his dead father's injunction, he produces an actual notebook, which, in Elizabethan England, probably took the form of a writing tablet (also referred to as 'tables'):

> My tables! Meet it is I set it down
> That one may smile and smile and be a villain –
>
> (1.5.107–8).

This is precisely the kind of saying, or maxim – known in early modern English as a 'saw' – that he has just pledged to obliterate from his memory. This is an extraordinary moment to decide to take notes, and it is one in which it is easy to see how Hamlet is an atypical hero of revenge tragedy and, in fact, not really a man of action at all. Shakespeare's other action heroes, such as Coriolanus, protagonist of the Roman tragedy of the same name or the stereotypically unbookish anti-hero, Hotspur of *1 Henry IV*, have no time or patience for reading and writing. Coriolanus plans to take revenge on Rome, the city that has banished him, and says, 'When blows have made me stay, I fled from words' (2.2.72). It is as if language is somehow inimical to martial engagement. Coriolanus won't shrink from a fight; he will confront his aggressor and stick with it in order to vanquish his opponent. Words are another matter – a more potent weapon from which he runs. (The last thing Coriolanus would do is whip out his notepad.) Instead of sweeping to revenge, Hamlet makes literal his own metaphor. Here is someone who lives more in his head than in the world.

If we examine this speech in its entirety, we will see that it begins with hesitation, but the hesitation is ethical in nature:

O all you host of heaven, O earth – what else? –
And shall I couple hell? O fie! Hold, hold, my heart,
And you, my sinews, grow not instant old
But bear me swiftly up. Remember thee?
Ay, thou poor ghost, whiles memory holds a seat
In this distracted globe. Remember thee?
Yea, from the table of my memory
I'll wipe away all trivial fond records,
All saws of books, all forms, all pressures past
That youth and observation copied there
And thy commandment all alone shall live
Within the book and volume of my brain
Unmixed with baser matter. Yes, by heaven,
O most pernicious woman,
O villain, villain, smiling damned villain,
My tables! Meet it is I set it down
That one may smile and smile and be a villain –
At least I am sure it may be so in Denmark.
So, uncle, there you are. Now to my word.
It is 'Adieu, adieu, remember me.'
I have sworn't.

(1.5.91–112)

'My word' is an oath but, it is also what the editor Harold Jenkins termed 'a watchword' – that is, far from turning away from bookish thoughts toward a plan of action in order to execute the promised revenge, Hamlet turns towards them.

Review

So far, we have considered what is distinctive about Shakespeare's writing in Q2 and why it is technically superior to the writing in Q1. We have also considered how Shakespeare manipulates the audience's expectations of revenge tragedy by allowing Hamlet to delay, and we have examined some of the central themes and images through which he does that. Shakespeare alters the pace of revenge so that, for example, while it is slowed in relation to Hamlet, it rushes murderously on in relation to Hamlet's mythical alter ego, Pyrrhus.

Writing matters

One very effective way to avoid feeling overwhelmed by the magnitude and complexity of *Hamlet* is to start small. Begin with an individual word, a line or a single unit of meaning rather than with a grandiose theory of the play. Large-scale, definitive theories about *Hamlet* tend to be wrong anyway (e.g. Hamlet is an allegorical figure for the German reformer Martin Luther, or Hamlet is really a woman – both of which have been advanced at various moments in the history of *Hamlet* criticism). This doesn't mean that you should avoid or repress your own big ideas about the play; it is simply that you are more likely to produce better and more convincing readings of the play as a whole if you begin with textual details and close analysis, which will allow you to move towards a more comprehensive appraisal of the play, rather than if you proceed the other way around.

By now, too, you should have seen one of the shorter *Hamlet* films. Now, move on to one (or better yet, two) of the longer versions. I recommend the *Hamlet* made for television movie (2009) directed by Gregory Doran, starring David Tennant (a.k.a. Doctor Who) and Kenneth Branagh's *Hamlet* (1996). Once you have more than one *Hamlet* under your belt, you can begin to compare and contrast them as you deepen your engagement with the play. Importantly, seeing *Hamlet* is not a substitute for reading the play, but in tandem with reading it, watching productions can help generate a plethora of critical questions as well as suggest specific areas of interest that you may want to pursue in terms of a longer writing project, such as a seminar paper or a longer essay.

Exercises

1   Imagine that Shakespeare's *Hamlet* never existed and that you have just written the script for a brand new movie. You are a genius (really), and you've written it in Elizabethan English, and it is exactly the same as the book we know as Shakespeare's *Hamlet*. The story has some similarities to a now-lost film from the 1930s, but otherwise it is completely new. The producers have a particular agenda in the face of a string of lacklustre flops: they are looking for a script with some really dynamic writing. Write a movie treatment for your script. What elements would you highlight to demonstrate the kind of energized writing that you know they are looking for? How would you show that the language of your script is integral to the plot rather than subservient to it?

2   In the Folio, Polonius's description of the players' repertoire reads as follows: 'tragedy, comedy, history, pastoral, pastorical-comical, historical-pastoral, tragical-historical, tragical-comical-historical-pastoral' (2.2.395–7). How does this alter the play's treatment of genre? Why do you think a revenge tragedy exhibits such self-consciousness about genre?

3   'You have not experienced Shakespeare until you have read him in the original Klingon', announces Chancellor Gorkon in the film *Star Trek VI: The Undiscovered Country*. The Klingons are the famous warrior race of *Star Trek*, easily identifiable by their distinctive, corrugated foreheads. Unsurprisingly, the most important text in the fictional Klingon

Shakespeare is *The Tragedy of Khamlet, Son of the Emperor Kronos*. Extending the joke, this text is published in the ostensibly 'original' Klingon, with a parallel English translation. This edition is based on fiction in that the Federation tried to claim the play as its own as part of their propaganda war against the Klingon Empire. This entertaining spoof – the invention of Marc Okrand – does, however, raise some fundamental questions about what constitutes the 'original' language of *Hamlet* and which are, in fact, topics of long-standing historical debate. This version also offers entertaining glosses on some of the more obsolete and obscure language in the play. Thus, 'Let the galled jade wince, our withers are unwrung' (3.2.236), in Shakespeare's text, a line about a clear conscience being impervious to guilt, becomes an English translation of the line in the ostensibly 'original' Klingon: 'We law abiders cannot be tortured by the mind sifter.' Similarly, 'he must build churches' (3.2.126) is rendered as 'he must name planets', while 'sledded Polacks' is taken as a reference to 'the Kinshaya in their armoured vehicles'.

Using the Klingon *Khamlet* as inspiration, choose one of the soliloquies in *Hamlet* and look it up in the early modern print versions of the text. There are facsimiles of both the Folio and Q2 online. Then, in consultation with your Arden edition, edit and gloss the text for yourself. Type out your edited text and explain how you arrived at it. In addition, add textual glosses. What would you explain and in what idiom would you explain it? Think about your intended audience here.

You can see a Klingon performance of 'To be or not to be' on YouTube: http://www.youtube.com/watch?v=CiRMGYQfXrs

4 In this chapter, we considered language in print, but we also discussed a version of *Hamlet* that is no longer extant, the *Ur-Hamlet*. Imagine you are clearing out your recently deceased great-grandmother's house. In a closet in the attic, you find, to your astonishment, a copy of the *Ur-Hamlet*. Your discovery settles once and for all the relationship between the play we have been reading and this text. What is in it? Was it written before or after the play as it has now come down to us? Feel free to describe the contents or to write a scene from the play.

5 Hamlet's final soliloquy 'How all occasions do inform against me' (4.4.31) is missing from the Folio text. What significance do you think this might have even if it were the only difference between Q2 and F? In answering this question try not to invent a theory about why it was omitted from the Folio in the first place. Instead, think about what meaning the play has in the absence of that soliloquy.

CHAPTER TWO

Language: forms and uses

In the last chapter we focused on how revenge structures the play as a whole and then examined specific passages in detail. This close analysis revealed Hamlet's disposition as that of an unlikely and reluctant avenger and showed how Shakespeare developed the revenge theme through other characters in the play, as well as through mythological vignettes. In this chapter, we will explore further strategies for analysing Shakespeare's language in depth and in detail by addressing how he worked with language as both the object and the implement of his writing. In particular, we will address two aspects of Shakespeare's language in *Hamlet*. The first part of this chapter will treat language as a theme in the play, while the second will focus primarily on the poetic and rhetorical techniques that make Shakespeare's language so powerful and effective. However, because these two elements are so closely connected, they cannot be treated as completely separate categories.

1. The theme of language: 'Words, words, words' (2.2.189)

There are *a lot* of words in *Hamlet* because it is, as we have noted, Shakespeare's longest play. Shakespeare purposely draws our attention to the obvious but crucial fact that when we read the text, we read 'Words, words, words.' After all, Shakespeare's language – and indeed all language – must consist of words. Whereas we tend to think *Hamlet* is made up of ideas – such as the ethics of revenge, the sovereignty of reason, the unknowability of death – the Renaissance understood, to paraphrase the nineteenth-century French poet Stéphane Mallarmé, that 'Poetry is not written with ideas, it is written with words' (Rylands, ix). To some degree, of course, this distinction is artificial: words *are* ideas, and the writer's ideas exist as words seen on the page or spoken on the stage. However, what Mallarmé was getting at is that, from the poet's point of view, coming before every other consideration is the way words are used and chosen. This is the craft of writing. When Shakespeare sat at his desk, quill in hand, he had to grapple with the technical aspects of dramatic poetry and prose – how to create rhythm, where to place pauses – not just those big ideas, such as, 'What piece of work is a man' (2.2.269). Yet, one of the fascinating things about *Hamlet* is that, as he composed the play, Shakespeare was clearly also interested in language *as an idea*. For all that, like Mallarmé, he still had to use words to express and develop language as a theme within the play. This is one of the self-reflexive aspects of *Hamlet* – its profound self-consciousness as dramatic poetry.

Language as an idea

One of the important ways through which Shakespeare makes language itself a conspicuous focal point of the play is the repetition of the word, 'word'. Horatio's obtrusively alliterative description of Hamlet's incoherence in the aftermath of his interview with the Ghost, for example, evokes the use of language as a flailing sword: 'These are but wild and whirling words, my Lord' (1.5.132). 'Word', in its various iterations, appears no fewer than 31 times in the Folio text. A word, of course, is the smallest unit of language that can be spoken or written in isolation and still bear semantic content – that is, still carry meaning. The Word (in the capitalized form and preceded by the definite article) was often used, and still is, as a synonym for Scripture, the Word of God. The widespread dissemination of the Word in English (as opposed to Latin) and in print was a brand new phenomenon in the sixteenth century. Famously, at the beginning of St. John's Gospel, the Greek word *logos* is translated as 'word': 'In the beginning was the Word, and the Word was with God, and the Word was God' (Jn 1.1) In the King James Bible, published shortly before Shakespeare's death, this passage continues in the form familiar to twenty-first century churchgoers: 'And the Word was made flesh, and dwelt among us' (Jn 1.14). The mysterious, divine word precedes all material reality, but it eventually manifests in the Christian mystery of the incarnation, whereby God became human. Almost any emphatic use of the word 'word' in *Hamlet*, no matter what the context, retains unshakable associations with divine mystery – that is, with something that can be intimated but can never be fully explained or understood.

This is arguably also true of language itself. For example, far beyond the business of practical communication, words remain puzzlingly isolated and detached from the things they designate. Instead of making meaning transparent, language also functions as a barrier at times and can be used (as it often is by villains like Claudius) as a means of deceit and subterfuge. Another facet of the mystery of language is that, although we use it to express ourselves, the words we speak do not originate within us. Words both are and are not our own. Maxims, aphorisms, adages (sayings) and what we would call clichés (which, in this period, are often referred to as 'saws') are the most obvious examples of this phenomenon. They are expressions that recognizably belong to the English (or other) language rather than to the particular speaker or writer who happens to be using them. Upon occasion, too, some of these sayings are attributed to a particular author. Famously,

'[F]oul deeds will rise / Though all the earth o'erwhelm them to men's eyes' (1.2.255–6) is from *The Adages of Erasmus*, the early sixteenth-century Dutch humanist. It is pat, familiar, and Shakespeare uses it to end the scene where Hamlet has determined that, 'though hell itself should gape' (1.2.243), he will speak with the Ghost. The adage allows Hamlet to vocalize a generalized sense of suspicion without making any specific accusation against Claudius for which, at this point in the play, he has no foundation.

Language barriers

In *Hamlet*, Shakespeare often highlights the tragic opacity of language. Far from facilitating communication, speech can become, whether deliberately or inadvertently, an impediment to it. In the following exchange, Hamlet's obfuscation is deliberate. He wants to wrong-foot Claudius, to trip him up. His witty manipulations of language serve both as a shield and as a weapon. Claudius makes the first foray into what should be a very ordinary conversational exchange: 'How *fares* our cousin Hamlet?' (3.2.88). In Hamlet's nonsensical prose reply to this innocuous inquiry about how things are going, he plays a game of puns with his bewildered uncle by taking 'fare' to mean food:

> HAMLET   Excellent, i'faith! Of the chameleon's dish
> – I eat the air, promise-crammed. You cannot feed the
> capons so.
> KING   I have nothing with this answer, Hamlet.
> These words are not mine.
> HAMLET   No, nor mine now my lord.

> (3.2.89–93)

Yet, Hamlet's conspicuous wordplay is far from playful. He uses language as a form of double-speak – speaking with a forked tongue so as to suggest the potentially divergent meanings of words and potentially even the instability of meaning itself. The wordplay on 'fare' is an instance of the rhetorical trope **antanaclasis**, which means to use the same word but with a different meaning. Hamlet's focus on food in this conversation harks back to the 'funeral baked meats' (1.2.179) that, as Hamlet bitterly complained to Horatio, were served at the wedding banquet for his mother and Claudius. The 'chameleon' here – the lizard that changes colour – was thought to live on air, and in this metaphor Hamlet is like a chameleon, thereby connecting him with the 'transformation' of both 'th'exterior' and 'the inward man' (2.2.5–6) that Claudius perceives him to have undergone. As Gertrude later asserts, 'words be made of breath' (3.4.195), as air and 'breath' constitute the material substance of vocalized words. Ostensibly the chameleon's food, air, wouldn't fatten a chicken. Yet Hamlet is 'promise-crammed' with it. He is force-fed and impotent like a capon – a castrated cockerel. This image suggests not only 'promise' in the sense of thwarted future potential, but also, and more literally, Hamlet's unfulfilled pledge to the Ghost. Of course, Claudius has no inkling of this, but the audience knows that the empty promise eating Hamlet is that of revenge. Indeed, revenge is very often referred to as something that needs to be fed. In *The Merchant of Venice*, Shylock seeks to 'feed my revenge' (3.1.49), and in *Coriolanus*, Volumnia declares, 'Anger's my meat' (4.2.50). Yet, because Hamlet is feeding on insubstantial 'air' that can never achieve a tangible outcome, he cannot make good on his promise to avenge his father's murder.

'[N]othing' in Claudius's line, 'I have nothing with this answer,' is also a key word not only in the above exchange but also throughout the play. 'Nothing' occurs four times in as many lines when Hamlet sees the Ghost in his mother's chamber (3.4.115–31), and as we will see in the next chapter, the word takes on specifically sexual connotations in Hamlet's exchanges with Ophelia before the players' performance of *The Murder of Gonzago*. For now, it is sufficient to note that Hamlet's verbal parries with Claudius argue for the insubstantial nature of words – specifically his promise to the Ghost – whereas Claudius anticipates (not unreasonably) a coherent and substantial outcome to his exchange with Hamlet. Language is something Claudius assumes he can own and possess. 'I *have* nothing' is a paradox since 'nothing' cannot be possessed. For Claudius, words should make sense, and they should belong to him like personal property: 'I have nothing with this answer, Hamlet. These words are not mine.' In replying, 'No, nor mine now my Lord,' Hamlet seems to be in agreement with Claudius that his words mean nothing. However, 'No, nor mine now my Lord' also means that once they have been uttered, words, being insubstantial like air, no longer belong – if they ever did – to the person who spoke them. Hamlet's riposte, like many of his ostensibly mad pronouncements, is proverbial. So these words are not (or not fully) either Hamlet's *or* Shakespeare's (Potter, 258).

Words and meanings

Throughout the play, Hamlet insists on the power and mystery of language in part by never letting anyone get away with using the word 'word' in a casual or completely innocuous sense. Take, for example, Guildenstern's very polite request to have a quick chat with Hamlet:

GUILDENSTERN Good, my lord, vouchsafe me a
  word with you.
HAMLET   Sir, a whole history.

         (3.2.288–90)

'[H]istory' denotes a story or a narrative, and thus Hamlet takes literally the figure of speech 'to have a word' with someone and amplifies it, or as early modern books on rhetoric would say, dilates it into much vaster proportions:

POLONIUS
                              – What do you read, my lord?
HAMLET   Words, words, words.
POLONIUS   What is the matter, my lord?
HAMLET   Between who?
POLONIUS   I mean the matter that you read, my lord.

                                              (2.2.188–92)

When Polonius asks, 'What is the matter, my lord?' he
wants to know the subject matter of the book that Hamlet
is reading, which is perhaps a book of satires – a 'satirical
rogue' (2.2.193). In another example of **antanaclasis** (using
the same word but with a different meaning), Hamlet deliberately misunderstands 'matter' to have an alternative meaning
(then common in Elizabethan English) – namely, a quarrel. At
this stage of the plot, Hamlet is arguably feigning insanity, but
the answer he delivers is literally true – he does read words,
but in saying so, he reveals as little as possible to Polonius.
'[T]he matter', in the sense of an altercation that would need
to be settled by a duel, anticipates the unfolding of action
in Act 5 and reminds the audience again of what's really the
'matter' with Hamlet – that he knows who killed his father.
Hamlet's initial response to the prying Polonius, who is trying
to discover the source of his alleged insanity, 'Words, words,
words,' really says that there is no meaning, no sense, no
semantic content to what he reads – that what he sees on the
page are merely empty signifiers. In his madness, whether it is
counterfeit or genuine, he makes nonsense of the page in front
of him. This conversation thus rehearses some of the main
themes of the play.

   Such a distinction between words and their meanings
occurs in Act 2, again in relation to the long-winded Polonius.
Impatient for him to get to the point, Gertrude demands:
'More matter with less art' (2.2.95). Hamlet himself also
reiterates this discrepancy between '[m]atter' and the words
used to express it:

> It is not madness
> That I have uttered. Bring me to the test
> And I the matter will reword, which madness
> Would gambol from.
>
> (3.4.139–42)

The image here is of a personified madness 'gambolling', or frolicking off from sense and coherence, without any determined direction or logical destination. Hamlet, however, aims to prove his sanity by extracting meaning ('the matter') from what his mother initially regards as nonsense.

This conjunction between 'words' and 'matter' – that is, substantive or material meaning, occurs numerous times in the play, but when it is used in relation to Gertrude, as when Hamlet warns her not to 'ravel all this matter out' (3.4.184), there is an inescapable association with the Latin word for mother, *mater*. This word reflects the ancient association of women with origins, nature, the physical body and raw material in contrast to men who are associated with civilization and culture. What's the matter with Hamlet? Arguably, the matter is his *mater*.

Word and deed: 'Suit the action to the word, the word to the action' (3.2.17–18)

For all that words entail serious consequences in *Hamlet*, words and deeds, whose vexed relationship constitutes a central theme of the play, regularly part company. What is 'out of joint' (1.5.186) in Denmark now that it is governed by a hypocritical and murderous king is that words and deeds are painfully dislocated from one another. Crucially, Hamlet does not follow through on the deed of revenge despite giving his word to do so until circumstances compel him to do so in Act 5.

Although in Hamlet's directions to the Players 'word' is used in its literal and most obvious sense, it is juxtaposed with 'gesture' so as to imply that word and action should go together. In acting, any disjunction between speech and movement is disastrous: 'Be not too tame neither, but let your own discretion be your tutor. Suit the action to the word, the word to the action' (3.2.16–18). '[A]ction' is precisely Hamlet's problem, which manifests as the discrepancy between his word (given to the Ghost) and the performance of the deed – revenge. At the beginning of the play, Horatio attests to the veracity of the guards' report that they have seen King Hamlet's ghost: 'each *word* made true and good' (1.2.209). Before Hamlet has actually seen the Ghost, its spectral reality can only be conveyed in words that are here understood to have the capacity to convey truth. These words are on the side of the angels as opposed to the demonic provenance Hamlet fears in relation to the Ghost's intelligence of his father's murder.

As we discussed in the previous chapter, when the Ghost himself appears and tells of his purgatorial sufferings, he speaks of the words that could indicate – though never fully describe – his condition: 'I could a tale unfold whose lightest word / Would harrow up thy soul' (1.5.15–16). Since to 'harrow' the soul is to uproot it, these soul-snatching words cannot be delivered to mortal ears. Hamlet's letter to Horatio, in which he promises to recount his aborted voyage to England, similarly suggests the power of language as well as its inadequacy. Remarkably, Hamlet's letter takes the same tone as the Ghost did in Act 1: '*I have words to speak in thine ear will make thee dumb. Yet are they much too light for the bore of the matter*' (4.6.23–5). In this metaphor, 'bore' refers to the calibre or gauge of a gun (as in a twelve-bore shotgun), and the idea here is that the ammunition is too light for the job at hand: 'Hamlet's words are seen as small bullets in a large cannon' (Thompson and Taylor, 392–3). In contrast, for Claudius, pricked by his conscience, words are merely a cosmetic veneer: 'my most painted word' (3.1.52). Here, it is not the words that are heavy, but what they hide, namely, the weight of murder – the 'heavy burden' of 'my deed' (3.1.52–3).

As illustrated in the following passage, words also carry weight when they are spoken as an oath – a vow or a pledge. '[S]worn' and 'word' have two consonants and a vowel in common, and they are often used in close proximity with one another, or with other words that share their syllables, such as 'now' and – as we shall see a bit later – 'sword'. Even though Hamlet suspects the Ghost of being a 'goblin damned' (1.4.40), he later tells Horatio, 'I'll take the Ghost's word for a thousand pound' (3.2.278–9). Hamlet's own word, however, is even more important than that of the Ghost's:

> Now to my word.
> It is 'Adieu, adieu, remember me.'
> I have sworn't.

> (1.5.110–12)

'Now' implies immediate or imminent action, but as critics often point out, Hamlet is actually swearing to remember and not to revenge. For all that, to swear an oath was a very serious form of verbal assurance, one that had profound implications in early modern England. The historian Edward Vallance describes an oath as 'a religious affirmation in which the swearer, by bringing God to witness his testimony, imprecates divine vengeance if it should prove false' (Vallance, 17). That oaths call down divine vengeance upon the heads of those who break them suggests that *Hamlet*'s revenge plot is undergirded by a cosmic scheme of divine retribution. Indeed, the Ghost's portrait of purgatorial perdition does nothing whatsoever to suggest the more benign dimensions of the deity in the Judeo-Christian tradition. God is wrathful at times, but he is also slow to anger and abounding in mercy. This merciful God does not make much of an appearance in the play. Had Hamlet actually succeeded in killing Claudius while he was at prayer, the deity might have shown mercy on him. However, for the murderer, Claudius, this potentially divine reprieve from perdition strikes a note of divine injustice rather than one of divine mercy.

Oaths of public office, private oaths to take revenge, or, indeed, marriage vows, are performative, which is to say that they have the status of action itself. So, for example, saying 'I do' is constitutive of marriage rather than simply a promise to love, honour and cherish in the future. (Once you say it in the context of the nuptial rite, you are married.) That is to say, oaths constitute deeds; they are not just hot air, nor are they just words. Perhaps this is why, despite his promise to avenge his father's murder, Hamlet is more focused on what he regards as his mother's abrogation of her wedding vows. When the Player Queen pledges that, should her husband die, she will not remarry, Hamlet comments with acerbic irony: 'O, but she'll keep her *word*' (3.2.225). Hamlet tells his mother that she 'makes marriage vows / As false as dicers' oaths (3.4.42–3). Her second marriage, according to Hamlet, makes her first one like the rash, empty and impetuous promise of a gambler playing dice – merely 'A rhapsody of words' (3.4.46). This is one of many instances in the play where we must pay attention to how the meaning of a word has changed. We may think, for example, of George Gershwin's musical composition, *Rhapsody in Blue*, but in early modern English the word 'rhapsody' sometimes had negative connotations.

Interestingly, too, because the hilt of a sword formed the shape of a cross, oaths were often pronounced upon swords. This was handy if you needed to swear an oath and you were not carrying a crucifix upon your person (as you would probably not have been doing in Protestant England where such religious appurtenances had fallen out of favour). Swords are implements of action and, in the early modern period, often signs of public office. Since every male actor in *Hamlet* would have been equipped with a sword, the oaths made upon them constitute actions performed on stage properties. After Hamlet has spoken with the Ghost, he makes his companions swear to secrecy, insisting that they repeat their oaths on a sword:

HAMLET
       Never make known what you have seen tonight.

HORATIO, MARCELLUS
    My lord, we will not.
HAMLET
    Nay, but swear't.
HORATIO   In faith, my lord, not I.
MARCELLUS
    Nor I, my lord, in faith.
HAMLET   Upon my sword.
MARCELLUS
    We have sworn, my lord, already.
HAMLET
    Indeed, upon my sword, indeed.
GHOST   (*Cries under the stage.*)
    Swear.

                                 (1.5.143–9)

In part because it has the solemnity of a religious rite, this can be a terrifying scene when performed in the theatre, with the Ghost repeatedly crying 'Swear' from below the stage. Interestingly, too, in early modern English, the 'w' in 'sword' was probably not silent. While 'sword' and 'lord' now share the same vowel sound, in Elizabethan English, the vowel in 'word' also shared this same pronunciation, whereas now, of course, it sounds more like 'wurd' or 'werd'. The sword, a symbol of decisive and potentially fatal action, serves as the guarantor of the word in the ritual of oath taking, and that is why Hamlet commands his companions to swear on it. It is a culturally accepted way of trying to bring words into alignment with actions. This also speaks to one of the problems associated with the referential facilities of language, namely that words possess the capacity of gesturing to something other than themselves. Words continually open up a breach between themselves and what they mean: the signifier and signified. Since there is always the danger that the one will get away from the other, oaths constitute a particular means of trying to keep them bound together.

When Claudius demands that Laertes kill Hamlet, we might expect words and deeds to be perfectly congruent with one another, but that is not the case. In the universe Claudius and Laertes inhabit, deeds and words operate not so much in concert with one another as they do in opposition to one another: the deed is 'more' than the word:

CLAUDIUS
> Hamlet comes back. What would you undertake
> To show yourself in *deed* your father's son
> More than in *words*?

LAERTES   To cut his throat i'th' church.

(4.7.122–4)

Laertes does not hesitate for a second here, and notice that the last part of the exchange consists of one iambic line shared between the two speakers. Shakespeare could have arranged these lines differently – as unshared lines. For example, he could have given Laertes a half-line pause for thought before having him decide to cut his adversary's throat. However, Shakespeare does not do that, and instead the shared line adeptly conveys Laertes' rapid-fire response. Further, this shared line lends a sense of conspiratorial complicity between the two men to have Hamlet murdered. Even though the audience may not consciously be aware of it, Shakespeare's technique here represents the way that conspiracies and covenants can emerge from spoken interaction.

Laertes is direct and unequivocal in his promise to revenge, and his second promise to Claudius in this conversation – the moment when he gives his *word* – is another instance of a shared line:

CLAUDIUS
> Requite him for your father.

LAERTES   I will do't.

(4.7.137)

Laertes' affirmation seals their compact of revenge in a straight-forward and clear-cut arrangement: the occasion, the time and the means of killing Hamlet are all set in place in this scene, contrasting with the vague arrangements negotiated between Hamlet and the Ghost in Act 1. Within Hamlet's more subtle and reflective sphere, however, there is a qualification about the correspondence between words and deeds that holds true whether the deeds in question are the gestures of an actor on a stage or revenge killings: 'Suit the action to the word, the word to the action, with this special observance – *that you o'erstep not the modesty of nature*' (3.2.16–18). In other words, in acting on the stage, just as in taking action in the world, there is a certain element of natural caution, a hesitation before the 'unnatural', which speaks not just to Hamlet's sense that a natural acting style is best, but also to his studied hesitance to pay back in kind the 'unnatural', (1.5.25) murder of his father. Perhaps this is why that although Hamlet seems poised to act when he says, '[n]ow to my word' (1.5.110) – his word is the prelude to three acts of hesitation.

Problem words: fat Hamlet

As you read the play, you will no doubt encounter many words that you do not know, perhaps because they are archaic and therefore no longer in everyday use. In such instances, the editorial glosses will be immensely helpful. However, there are some words, as in the example of 'rhapsody' discussed above, where the Elizabethan meaning has become obsolete but not the word itself. Another well-known example from the play is the word 'rivals', which is used in relation to the soldiers on watch on the battlements. When Barnardo speaks of '[t]he rivals of my watch' (1.1.11), he does not mean opponents as we might expect but, rather, the opposite – his fellow sentinels.

Sometimes, however, we have to live with the fact that we really do not know what Shakespeare meant. Take the word 'fat' (5.2.269), for example. Before we address its meaning, we might note that this is a monosyllabic Anglo-Saxon word, as opposed to the more complex Latinate words that were also a part of Shakespeare's linguistic inheritance. A Latinate word for 'fat' would be 'adipose', but Shakespeare does not use it in *Hamlet* or, indeed, anywhere else in the canon. It is rather surprising that in the critical tradition that has grown up around the play, 'fat' has proved to be a word of vigorously contested meaning. In the duelling scene, Act 5, scene 2, in response to Claudius's utterly dishonest assertion that Hamlet will win, Gertrude says, 'He's fat and scant of breath' (5.2.269). The problem here is that a fat Hamlet does not comport with our idea of Hamlet as an agile tragic hero or as a Renaissance prince. Thompson and Taylor point out that critics have not wanted 'fat' to mean 'overweight' (453). Is Gertrude really saying that Hamlet's girth makes his victory unlikely? Is he struggling in the contest because he is heavy and winded with exertion? Horatio certainly seems to think Hamlet is the weaker contestant but he gives no indication that this is because Hamlet is overweight. When the contest is announced, he simply and unequivocally tells Hamlet, 'You will lose, my lord' (5.2.187).

There is quite a lot of 'fat' in *Hamlet*, and when the Ghost uses the word after Hamlet has said that he wants immediately to 'sweep to my revenge' (1.5.31), he means bloated:

> I find thee apt.
> And duller shouldst thou be than the fat weed
> That roots itself in ease on Lethe wharf
> Wouldst thou not stir in this.

$$(1.5.31–4)$$

In classical mythology Lethe is the river of forgetfulness in the underworld. While Hamlet never forgets his promise, he does not act on it. Is he, therefore, by Act 5, in fact as dull as a fat weed growing by the river? Certainly, 'fat' is meant in the literal sense (assuming that there is any other) elsewhere in the play, such as when Hamlet says to Claudius, 'We fat all / creatures else to fat us, and we fat ourselves for maggots. / Your fat king and your lean beggar is but variable / service, two dishes but to one table' (4.3.21–4), and when he describes 'the fatness of these pursy times' (3.4.151). Hamlet regrets not having already killed Claudius and fed his guts to local birds of prey, thus making them fat: 'ere this / I should ha' fatted all the region kites / With this slave's offal' (2.2.513–15).

In contrast, an argument for a thinner Hamlet might be found in his clothes. There are sartorial associations between Hamlet's 'suits of woe' (1.2.86), his 'customary suits of solemn black' (1.2.78) and his 'inky cloak' (1.2.77) with the carnival figure, Jack of Lent, who represents the Lenten abstinence from meat, practised for a full six weeks prior to Easter Sunday in early modern England. If we subscribe to this connotation, Hamlet is the lean antithesis of all that is associated with meat and plenty. After all, flesh is what carnival celebrates. The etymological derivation of carnival is *carne*, which is Latin for 'meat' (Burke, 265).

However, if Hamlet is fat, he has at least been working out: 'Since he [Laertes] went into France I have been in continual practice' (5.2.188–9). As in many places in the play, there is no easy way to resolve the problem of meaning here, which can only be decisively achieved in the theatre – where Hamlet is typically svelte and athletic. We must confront our own cultural prejudices about weight and consider that what we take 'fat' to mean may change our ideas about Hamlet's prospects for taking revenge as well as our understandings of his identity as a tragic protagonist.

Who is speaking, and to whom? Soliloquy and aside

One of the most important dramatic techniques Shakespeare deploys to make Hamlet seem not just like a character but also like an actual person is that he gives us insight into his inner thought process via soliloquies. In other words, we hear Hamlet talking, or thinking, to himself.

Derived from the Latin word *soliloquium*, soliloquy literally means 'speaking alone'. As Darlene Farabee points out, 'A soliloquy is a very distinctive form of dramatic language, representing not the speech of a character, but rather his or her *thoughts*.' 'By convention,' continues Farabee, 'in early modern plays characters speaking in soliloquy tell the truth' (Farabee, 7). There are twelve soliloquies in *Hamlet*, but not all of them belong to the play's eponymous prince; Claudius has two, Ophelia has one and there is a soliloquy in the play-within-the-play. Asides are more numerous than soliloquies and they constitute the convention whereby a character's speech is ostensibly unheard by some or all of the other characters on stage. However, the distinction between soliloquies and asides is not always clear and the question of who is addressed by them is far from straightforward.

There are moments in the play when Hamlet's solitude is emphasized, such as the beginning of the soliloquy, 'O, what a rogue and peasant slave am I!' (2.2.485), a line that Hamlet prefaces by stating, 'Now I am alone' (2.2.484). This assertion may suggest that Hamlet is not addressing the audience, but, rather, that they overhear him. There is, however, a good deal of critical controversy about when and whether soliloquies and asides are spoken directly to the audience and, indeed, about whether other characters on stage are supposed to hear what is being spoken in them. For example, performance tradition makes Hamlet's withering rebuttal to Claudius's attempt to make Hamlet 'my son' (1.2.64) an aside. This is the famous moment in the play when Hamlet responds, 'A little more than kin, and less than kind' (1.2.65). However, this is not an aside in any of the extant texts of the play (McEvoy, 78). If this is not an aside, then Hamlet's sarcasm here constitutes a much more direct confrontation with Claudius than we might otherwise assume to be the case given his reluctance openly to accuse the King of his father's murder. Another point of controversy is Hamlet's most famous soliloquy, 'To be, or not to be' (3.1.55–87). It is spoken just as Polonius and Claudius have hidden themselves to eavesdrop on him. Ophelia, however, is still on stage and remains so throughout Hamlet's speech. Although this speech is traditionally numbered among Hamlet's soliloquies, in terms of the plot at least, he is not actually alone but on stage with three other characters.

Aside

As in the case of the following four lines spoken by Gertrude, editors do not always agree as to whether particular speeches are asides or soliloquies:

> To my sick soul, as sin's true nature is,
> Each toy seems prologue to some great amiss,
> So full of artless jealousy is guilt
> It spills itself in fearing to be spilt.

> (4.5.17–20)

Some scholars, such as Marvin Rosenberg, argue that this speech is Gertrude's 'one pure soliloquy' (Rosenberg, 760). In the Arden edition, however, Gertrude's speech in Act 4 scene 5 is an aside, rather than a soliloquy, because it occurs just as Ophelia enters the stage. The contrast between these two forms – the aside and the soliloquy – is instructive because, despite certain obvious similarities, these are distinct dramatic strategies that achieve different theatrical effects. Soliloquies are typically quite revealing, whereas asides, such as the ones we will examine below, reveal a disjunction – sometimes chasm-wide – between what characters say and what they do not disclose.

Gertrude's aside may represent her private ruminations in the wake of Hamlet's verbal assault on her in the closet scene in Act 3 scene 4, or it may be addressed to the audience. In the original text of Q2, each of these lines is prefaced by a quotation mark to signify that this pair of couplets consists of commonplace expressions, or **sententiae**. Thus:

'To my sick soul, as sin's true nature is,
'Each toy seems prologue to some great amiss,
'So full of artless jealousy is guilt,
'It spills itself in fearing to be spilt.

(4.5.17–20)

This suggestion that Gertrude is speaking words that are not completely her own is further emphasized by the sense of artifice induced by the rhymes: 'is'/ 'amiss' (probably homonyms in Elizabethan pronunciation) and 'guilt'/ 'spilt'. The first couplet here begins with the alliterative 's' – 'sick', 'soul', 'sin' – and culminates in 'amiss'. The line is structured so that the feared but as yet outwardly unmanifest consequences of sin become fully realized and descend upon the speaker in that final double 's'. This is not, of course, something that the audience would necessarily be conscious of during a performance, but whether or not we pick up on the technique used, we still *feel* something of Gertrude's inner turmoil. We experience with her that inchoate sense of being sick, sinful and guilty, and this impact is the result of Shakespeare's careful patterning of language.

The second couplet above takes us to what we would really like to know – the degree of Gertrude's guilt. However, the nature of the commonplace is such that it works to evade the specific, individual truth of Gertrude's culpability because it speaks only to generalities rather than to particulars. A great deal hangs not only on what we take these lines to mean, but also on whether Gertrude is talking to herself or to the audience. That these are sententiae means that they are at one remove from the direct expression of Gertrude's thought. That is to say, since she is quoting well-worn expressions, they provide a tantalizingly opaque window into her conscience. We are not really much the wiser as to the question of whether she conspired with Claudius in the murder, or whether her remorse results from her sexual liaison with him. We cannot even know for sure whether Gertrude is talking about

Claudius or about herself. The lines are deliberately – even maddeningly – ambiguous. Through them, Shakespeare whets the audience's appetite for the truth, and he is able to do so via a particular dramatic form, the aside, which we hope will deliver it. Such expectations are thwarted, and we are hooked, avidly awaiting some form of concrete information that the play withholds.

Not all asides in *Hamlet* are so cryptic. Polonius is given several asides in the play because he is Elsinore's chief spy and eavesdropper. Some of his most famous include, 'Though this be madness, yet there is method in't' (2.2.202–3) and 'Still on my daughter' (2.2.345), both of which are pithy observations about Hamlet's 'antic' discourse. However, Polonius also unwittingly provokes an aside from Claudius when he remarks that people often cover their wickedness with a semblance of piety: 'How smart a lash that speech doth give my conscience!' (3.1.49). For the first time, the audience is allowed a glimpse into the inner Claudius, who is, perhaps surprisingly, possessed of a conscience and who suffers guilt for his crime, which potentially creates sympathy with him along with further evidence and reminder of his guilt.

Asides work to structure the play's language by creating theatrical dynamism. They tell us about the motives and emotions of characters and about the relationships between characters as in, for example, the fraught exchanges between Rosencrantz and Guildenstern in Act 2 scene 2, when Hamlet demands to know whether they have been sent by Claudius:

ROSENCRANTZ (*aside to Guildenstern*) What say you?
HAMLET (*aside*) Nay then, I have an eye of you.

(2.2.255–6)

Rosencrantz is trying to assess whether prevarication would be politic at this point because, of course, he and Guildenstern are visiting Hamlet at the behest of Claudius. What should they say? Should they lie or tell the truth? Hamlet's own aside immediately follows. He knows their game; he has an eye on them. These three characters are close enough onstage to be in conversation and yet, for a moment, they are avoiding the confrontation that would ensue from open and direct address. These asides thus work to emphasize the insidious and almost intimate way Rosencrantz and Guildenstern seek to deceive Hamlet.

Talking to himself

Unlike some of the characters in Shakespeare's other plays, such as *Othello*'s Iago, whose soliloquies address the audience in a very direct way, Hamlet really does seem to be talking to himself. Indeed, there is arguably little in the way of direct address to the audience in *Hamlet*. Hamlet's soliloquies permit the audience to overhear his self-addressed expressions of private thoughts and feelings. Arguably, these speeches increase the sense of an inscrutable inner life: what he describes to the prying Rosencrantz and Guildenstern as 'the heart of my mystery' (3.2.357–8). For all that, there is also a sense of urgency about wanting to disclose and unburden the self by means of unfettered speech. This is especially significant since Hamlet's very first soliloquy ends with the anguish of wanting to speak freely and yet he is unable to do so within the political context of Elsinore: 'But break, my heart, for I must hold my tongue' (1.2.159). This is what Shakespeare describes in Sonnet 66 as being 'made tongue-tied by authority' (*l.* 9). While here Hamlet has something in common with Shakespeare's deposed Richard II, who says 'My heart is great, but it must break with silence' (2.1.228), he has even more in common, perhaps surprisingly, with the truculent Katherine of *The Taming of the Shrew*:

My tongue will tell the anger of my heart,
Or else my heart concealing it will break,

And, rather than it shall, I will be free
Even to the uttermost, as I please, in words.

(4.3.79–82)

Katherine's speech is, of course, not a soliloquy, and what restricts her speech is her gender, rather than the kind of political predicament by which the Prince is hamstrung. For all that, her lines convey a similar sense that language and the particular restraints imposed on it shape and constrain human identity. In a lighter vein, when Hamlet welcomes the Players to Elsinore, in reference to the actor playing the female role, he asserts, 'the Lady shall say her mind freely or the blank verse shall halt for't' (2.2.289–90). In other words, her lines should be as Polonius says a little later in commendation of Hamlet's own recitation – 'well spoken – with good accent and good discretion' (2.2.404–5). If the actor does not speak with fluid expression, the verse will sound stilted, or out of rhythm. However, there is also the sense that the female character will be allowed free and perhaps uninterrupted speech. If she is not, the metre of the verse will be lame or halting. It is particularly important, then, that soliloquies represent freedom of expression and thought in a culture that did not typically condone them (as we saw in the last chapter on pages 41–2). Early modern England tended to regard liberty of both thought and expression, or licentious speech, as dangerous, and therefore as something to be forcibly suppressed.

First soliloquy

The strategies used for examining the language of the first soliloquy in terms of tone, imagery, diction, theme and so forth can be applied to any and all of the soliloquies in *Hamlet*, and indeed to any passage that you want to focus on for close reading. First, consider where the passage is placed in the play and what happens before and after it. Such considerations allow you to see how the play's architecture

– its structure – works to develop themes and characters. In relation to soliloquies, it is especially important to consider how far off or, conversely, how closely integrated, the speech is to the surrounding action and language of the play. In the case of the first soliloquy in *Hamlet*, poised between Claudius's reprimand for Hamlet's immoderate grief and Horatio's revelation that King Hamlet's ghost has been seen on the castle's battlements, the emphasis is on Hamlet's emotional distance from his father's other surviving relatives. Through Hamlet's classical references in this speech – to Hyperion (the sun god), Hercules (the son of Zeus and a figure of prodigious strength), Niobe (who was punished by the gods with the loss of all her children who remained unburied for nine days) and the satyr (the mythical figure who is part-man and part-goat) – we get a glimpse into the learned mind of a Renaissance prince. Classical references become more important as the play progresses, especially when the fall of Troy becomes a potent parallel for events in Elsinore:

O that this too too sallied flesh would melt,
Thaw and resolve itself into a dew,
Or that the Everlasting had not fixed
His canon 'gainst self-slaughter. O God, God,
How weary, stale, flat and unprofitable
Seem to me all the uses of this world!
Fie on't, ah, fie, 'tis an unweeded garden
That grows to seed, things rank and gross in nature
Possess it merely. That it should come thus:
But two months dead – nay not so much, not two –
So excellent a king, that was to this
Hyperion to a satyr, so loving to my mother
That he might not beteem the winds of heaven
Visit her face too roughly. Heaven and earth,
Must I remember? Why, she should hang on him
As if increase of appetite had grown
By what it fed on. And yet within a month
(Let me not think on't – Frailty, thy name is Woman),

A little month, or e'er those shoes were old
With which she followed my poor father's body,
Like Niobe, all tears. Why, she –
O God, a beast that wants discourse of reason
Would have mourned longer – married with my uncle,
My father's brother (but no more like my father
Than I to Hercules). Within a month,
Ere yet the salt of most unrighteous tears
Had left the flushing in her galled eyes,
She married. O most wicked speed! To post
With such dexterity to incestuous sheets,
It is not, nor it cannot come to good;
But break, my heart, for I must hold my tongue.

$$(1.2.129–59)$$

Up to this point, the audience has not heard much from
Hamlet, only his cryptic aside to Claudius and a brief
response to Gertrude's injunction to remove his mourning
garments – to 'cast thy nighted colour off' (1.2.68). Now,
we discover what he really thinks and how he really feels.
Thus, the soliloquy serves an important dramatic function
in terms of the revelation of Hamlet's melancholy, a medical
condition understood similarly to the way depression is
today. Melancholy was widely written about at the time, the
most famous book on the subject being Robert Burton's *The
Anatomy of Melancholy* (1621).

The first lines of this soliloquy express the desire for
non-being, for the vaporization of the 'sallied flesh' – assailed
or beset by gruelling circumstances – the distraught life of the
physical body. The language used is that of alchemical transformation in which substances melt and dissolve. '[M]elt' and
'thaw' echo the same idea, except that 'thaw' refers to a frozen
substance (such as ice as opposed to, say, melting butter). In
the Folio, the adjective used for 'flesh' is not 'sallied' but 'solid',
which suggests that Hamlet's desired dissolution is impossible.
Given the unlikelihood of spontaneous evaporation into 'a

dew', suicide is the next logical step. The weed-ridden world described by Hamlet is the direct antithesis of the lush garden described in Genesis in the Bishop's Bible (1568) as: '[O]ut of the ground made the Lord God to grow every tree, that was faire to sight' (Gen. 2.9). Unlike Eden, this uncontrolled and unnatural proliferation constitutes an aberration in nature. This is a place where only stinking, 'rank' vegetation flourishes. Hamlet uses 'rank' again in relation to his mother's bed: 'the rank and sweat of an enseamed bed' (3.4.90). Especially since the iambic line requires an emphasis on the last syllable, 'enseamèd' again suggests insemination – a bed saturated with semen, even though editors typically gloss this word as meaning 'greasy'. In the first soliloquy, from the general desire for self-annihilation to the disgust with life and all that attends it in the world, the audience becomes privy to the specific causes of Hamlet's dejection. '[S]eed', 'rank' and 'gross' – while they refer directly to Hamlet's analogy of the world as a foul garden – prepare the way, ideationally, for the sexual transgressions performed on 'incestuous sheets' (1.2.157) that will preoccupy him for the remainder of the play.

What supports the questionable claim that his mother's remarriage is indeed incestuous is Hamlet's assertion that Gertrude has 'married with my uncle, / My father's brother' (1.2.151–2). Even though Henry VIII had done just that when, in 1509, he married his dead brother Arthur's widow, Catherine of Aragon, there remained biblical prohibitions against marrying a deceased sibling's spouse. And, indeed, the 'incestuous sheets' of that royal marriage were literally brought in as evidence when Henry sought to divorce Catherine to marry Anne Boleyn (Elizabeth I's mother). Catherine aimed to show that her marriage with the sickly Arthur had never been consummated. Further she produced a bloodstained sheet from her wedding night with Henry by way of evidence of hymenal rupture and thus proof that she had been a virgin when she married him. Because Elizabethans were required by law to attend church on Sunday, they were necessarily familiar with the regulations about intermarriage from the tables of consanguinity (blood relation) that hung in England's churches and that appeared in the government-mandated Book of Common Prayer as a 'Table of Kindred and Affinity'. We will see in Chapter Three that Hamlet has a lot to say about bedding in connection with incest in Act 3 scene 4. For now, it is enough to note that Hamlet's comparison of his father with Claudius works to intensify the association between the latter and aberrant sexual behaviour.

According to his son, King Hamlet was like the sun god, Hyperion, and was an extraordinarily protective, 'perfect' husband to Gertrude. The hyperbolic image here is of a deity who forbids the wind to roughen his wife's complexion. As Hamlet describes it, King Hamlet's behaviour towards his wife was devoid of sexual implications – he merely protected her from the elements that threatened her beauty, like the 'Rough winds' that 'shake the darling buds of May' (*l*. 3) in Sonnet 18. Gertrude, in contrast, is understood to have – or at least pretended to have had – a specifically and ever-increasing carnal desire for her husband. '[I]ncrease' and 'grown' in the same line speak again to issues of generation, as in the biblical injunction to 'increase and multiply'. '[G]rown' is also poten- tially homonymic with 'groan' in terms of both the sound effects of copulation and the groans of childbirth. Hamlet tells Ophelia in Act 3 scene 2 that sex 'would cost you a groaning' (3.2.242). These associations with pregnancy indicate that Gertrude may be still of childbearing age. Clearly, however, in the apparently 30 years since his birth, Gertrude has not produced a sibling for Hamlet despite her apparent love for his father. Yet, 'within a month' (1.2.145), she has coupled with his uncle who is represented as the half-man, half-goat – the priapic satyr – a figure often depicted with a monstrous, erect phallus and who is characterized principally by his sexual appetite.

Although it is in fact four months since Hamlet's father died, time becomes telescoped as he muses on the 'most wicked speed' (1.2.156) of his mother's remarriage. He begins with 'two months' and immediately reduces the period to less than two – 'not two' (1.2.138). The interval is even further diminished – 'within a month' (1.2.145), '[a] little month' (1.2.147). Albeit from Hamlet's faulty calculations, we learn for the first time how short the period has been between his father's death and his mother's wedding. In the previous scene in the Danish court, the audience was completely ignorant of this fact. Thus, his mother's claim that Hamlet's grief was inappropriately protracted seemed plausible: 'Do not for ever with thy vailed lids / Seek for thy noble father in the dust' (1.2.70–1). Now, it becomes clear that the problem was not Hamlet's lingering grief but his mother's precipitately terminated mourning. However, the audience does not yet know how far Hamlet's sense of time is off. That information awaits us, occurring just before the performance of *The Mousetrap*. Hamlet tells Ophelia, 'my father died within's two hours!' (3.2.120), only to be corrected by her: 'Nay, 'tis twice two months, my lord' (3.2.121).

Hamlet's focus on the indecently truncated mourning period is understandable, but that it is measured in months, and that those months are repeated in conjunction with his mother's 'increase' and 'groan', connotes the cycles of human fertility – menstruation and pregnancy – especially since the words 'within a month' (the interval of the menses) directly precede Hamlet's misogynist depth charge: 'Frailty, thy name is Woman' (1.2.146). Women and animals were regularly elided in early modern discourse as being ruled by their imaginations and being devoid of reason. Women were also understood to be the more lascivious sex, subject to the desires of the body in a way that men – who were allegedly more fully endowed with rational capacities – were not. Negative generalizations about the nature of women are invariably manifestations of a pervasive early modern cultural prejudice against them, but three consecutive lines ending in 'grown/groan', 'month' and 'Woman' imply a more specific substratum of ideas about female reproduction. They further indicate that Hamlet's sense of temporality is formed entirely in relation to his mother.

A fascinating detail of the first soliloquy is Hamlet's almost fetishistic consideration of his mother's shoes. The sense here is that she remarried before the presumably new shoes she wore to the funeral procession had worn out: 'e'er those shoes were old / With which she followed my poor father's body' (1.2.47–8). As editors typically note, these are cloth shoes – the kind mentioned in John Webster's *The Duchess of Malfi* (1614) in which 'foot-cloth' is renewed 'with the fall of the leaf' (2.1.47–9). In that funeral procession wearing those shoes, Gertrude was 'Like Niobe, all tears', the mythological figure whose grief turned her into a weeping statue. It is not so much that Hamlet wishes his mother's life to be held permanently in suspended animation, but rather that he objects to the haste with which she has bedded Claudius. The animating qualities conveyed by the words 'speed' and 'dexterity' are the antitheses of the immovable Niobe.

Rather than being simply brief and isolated, classical references such as Hyperion, the satyr, Niobe and Hercules create a rich mythological foundation for Hamlet's narrative of abbreviated funeral rites and hasty nuptials. Hamlet's father figures as Hyperion, a celestial emblem of divinely ordained sovereignty, as well as Hercules, the classical image of supreme strength. Hamlet's mother figures – albeit briefly – as Niobe, while Claudius is the satyr. At first glance, in this soliloquy, Hamlet himself seems situated beneath the mythological deities as an unremarkable mortal. However, for Shakespeare's favourite poet, Ovid, in Arthur Golding's translation of his *Metamorphoses* (1567), Niobe's transformation is described not only as petrification but also as liquefaction: 'There upon a mountaines top / She weepeth still in stone. From the drerie teares do drop' (6.394–5). Niobe is the first of the play's female mourners. She will be succeeded in Act 3 by Hecuba, who is referred to in *Titus Andronicus* as 'Hecuba of Troy', who 'Ran mad for sorrow' (4.1.20–1). This emotional connection between mother and son (both Niobes) is further developed when Claudius explains that 'The Queen his mother / Lives almost by his looks' (4.7.12–13).

However, Hamlet resembles not only the mythological Niobe but also the nymph, Canens, who dies of grief for her beloved Picus:

At last, attenuated so by grief
That in her bones the marrow turned to water,
She melted down and vanished on the breezes

(Ovid, 14.606–8, trans. Charles Martin)

Such watery, feminine mourning also anticipates the grief-stricken Ophelia's fate, since she also melts into water. Like the renowned vocalist Canens, singing is also the métier of Ophelia's mourning. Hamlet's resemblance to these Ovidian female mourners perhaps explains why, by his own admission, he looks nothing like his father. The repellent Claudius does not look like Hamlet's father, but neither does Hamlet who is 'no more like my father / Than I to Hercules' (1.2.152–3). That Claudius does not resemble his deceased sibling is not particularly surprising, especially from the invariably biased perspective of his aggrieved nephew. Hamlet will harp on this disparity between his father and his uncle again in the closet scene when he compares their portraits. However, what is striking here is the dissimilarity between father and son within the context of his disquisition on Gertrude's sexual incontinence. Hercules is a figure of heroic physical proportions, and that Hamlet bears no resemblance to him might suggest a momentary uncertainty about his own paternity despite his frequent and otherwise confident assertions that the deceased king of Denmark was indeed 'my father'. The play does not encourage us to doubt this truth, but for one flickering second, we might wonder just how 'sullied' or 'sallied' Hamlet's flesh really is – not by his own misconduct, but by his mother's. Hamlet's sense of identity, however, has become scrambled by the sudden, incestuous rearrangement of his familial relationships, and as he tells Horatio when emerging from this reverie, 'I do forget myself' (1.2.161). The order and coherence of his lived experience, which are the constituents of a cohesive sense of self, are all undone by this unorthodox marriage. 'I do forget myself' follows the soliloquy's 'Must I remember?' (1.2.143), preparing the audience for the Ghost's injunction, which arrives as a crescendo in the last scene of this opening act: 'remember me' (1.5.91).

Thinking out loud

In the 'Preface to the First Edition of *Poems*' (1853), Matthew Arnold referred to the soliloquies of the Elizabethan stage as 'the dialogue of the mind with itself' (Arnold, 654). Other than Hamlet, the only character in the play whose inner life is thus revealed is the guilt-ridden Claudius. We do glimpse Ophelia's inner life in her madness, but these moments are typically inappropriate public revelations of her torment. Indeed, she offers a remarkable psychosexual portrait of someone suffering from abject grief and inconsolable loss. Shakespeare does not explicitly reveal Gertrude's interiority in the manner of soliloquy, in part because to do so would be to undo some of the play's greatest riddles: what did she know about the murder, and when did she know it? Is she indeed an adulteress, and if so, did she conspire with Claudius in the murder of King Hamlet? More than that, however, Gertrude is a character seen primarily from the outside. We see her through Hamlet's eyes when she tells him her heart is 'cleft … in twain' (3.4.154), and we see her as the object of her deceased husband's inordinate, uxorious love. In her exquisitely lyrical description of Ophelia's death – 'There is a willow grows askant the brook / That shows his hoary leaves in the glassy stream' (4.7.164–5) – there are remarkable glimmers of what is inside that cleft heart of hers, but she does not share her private thoughts directly with the audience. Generations of audiences and readers have identified with and admired Hamlet in part because we know him better than any of the play's other characters, and this is so primarily because of his soliloquies. The first soliloquy in *Hamlet*, as we have noted, is before he learns of his father's murder – 'O that this too too sallied flesh would melt' (1.2.129) – and the last of his eight soliloquies occurs in Act 4 – 'How all occasions do inform against me' (4.4.31) – when there is, perhaps astonishingly, almost a third of the play left to run.

2. The craft of language

The next section will examine the nature of dramatic verse in Shakespeare's theatre and how it is distinguished from the play's prose in terms of both form and function. We will also consider the impact of silence not only as an important theme in the play, but also, paradoxically, as an integral part of the play's representation of language.

Blank verse

While we tend to assume that the English language has always been an ideal vehicle for literary expression, this is not, in fact, the case. Edmund Spenser, author of the great Elizabethan epic *The Faerie Queene* (1590–6), famously demanded in a letter to his good friend, Gabriel Harvey, 'Why a [in] God's name, may not we, as else the Greeks, have the kingdom of our own language?' (Helgerson, 1). Despite Chaucer's literary achievement in the fourteenth century, English continued to be thought of as a rather crude and unwieldy language, a mish-mash of other tongues and not very well suited to poetry. In the course of the second half of the sixteenth century, all that changed as writers at last established the English language as one just as capable of lyrical eloquence as the ancient literary languages of Greek and Latin.

This is important because Shakespeare wrote *Hamlet* in the wake of some of the most monumental achievements of English verse in the 1590s, and indeed, the end of the sixteenth century saw poets demonstrate unequivocally that they had overcome problems that had bedevilled English verse even as late as the 1580s. This was achieved in part by the discovery that the iamb (a metrical unit in which one unstressed syllable is followed by a stressed syllable) and the pentameter line were best suited for English speech. Blank verse, or unrhymed iambic pentameter – with its ten syllables and five stresses – was a poetic form, then, that English authors had struggled to achieve.

All poetic language must be close enough to conversational speech to be plausible and sufficiently elevated enough from it to be understood as poetry, as art. Poets have always walked a tightrope between these two extremes, but in dramatic poetry the precept famously articulated by T. S. Eliot is paramount: '[P]oetry must not stray too far from the ordinary everyday language which we use and hear' (Eliot, 21).

Metre, rhyme and elevated diction are the most obvious (though not the only) ways of differentiating poetry from workaday language, and the linguistic registers of *Hamlet* include song at one end of the linguistic spectrum and prose at the other. Song is the point at which lyricism quite deliberately parts company with speech, while prose, no matter how artful or carefully wrought, is the point at which language becomes more closely coincident with non-dramatic speech. More fundamentally, however, *Hamlet* considers silence – especially the silence of death, which is beyond all speech and writing, as that which frames all forms of utterance.

Shakespeare and Marlowe

Christopher Marlowe was the first great innovator of dramatic verse, and he succeeded in turning the five-stress, ten-syllable line into what another great contemporary of Shakespeare, Ben Jonson, called 'Marlowe's mighty line'. This English metrical form first appeared in print in the Earl of Surrey's translation of Virgil's *Aeneid* (c. 1554). Marlowe went on to develop iambic pentameter for the theatre in his blockbuster tragedy, *Tamburlaine* (c. 1587), the story of a lowly shepherd who became the most powerful man on earth. Such a hero required the kind of language that would express his prowess, although this also involved, as Jonson also noted in his *Discoveries* (1641), 'scenical strutting and furious vociferation' (*l.* 789–92). Marlowe's dramatic verse was powerful, then, but as Thomas Nashe complained in his preface to Robert Greene's romance *Menaphon*, it could sound like ranting. For Nashe, Marlowe was one of those:

> idiot Art-masters, that intrude themselves to our ears as the Alchemists of eloquence, who (mounting on the stage of arrogance) think to out-brave better pens with the swelling bombast of bragging blank verse (3:311).

Nashe did not mention Marlowe by name, but his 'Art-master' jibe would have identified Marlowe, who had an MA from Cambridge as one of the playwrights he was attacking. '[T]he swelling bombast of bragging blank verse' cleverly parodies the kind of oversized, over-the-top language that bludgeons the hearer with its alliterative thump. Despite being wedded to ornate hyperbole himself, Nashe further complained about 'the spacious volubility of a drumming decasyllabon' – that is, the thud of the iamb with its second syllable stress, which, if it is executed with monotonous, metronomic regularity, indeed begins to sound like a drum or a hammer. This problem arose when playwrights aimed to capture what Hamlet called 'enterprises of great pitch and moment' (3.1.85), the height and depth of human experience at moments of utmost significance. George T. Wright emphasizes this point as follows: 'Metrical lines are mathematical, musical, architectural constructs, and iambic pentameter is a numerical syllabic and accentual form charged by the technical achievements mainly of sixteenth-century poets to address and embody the largest human issues' (Wright, 289). By means of irregular lines and lines with unstressed endings, however, Shakespeare tends to modulate the effects of what Jonson and Nashe railed against.

Subtle versification of the kind that Shakespeare specialized in was not, however, the only effective theatrical language. Indeed, Hamlet makes it clear that he enjoys the self-conscious artifice of dramatic verse typically associated with Marlowe. The speech that Hamlet asks the Players who arrive in Elsinore to perform is indebted to Marlowe's *Dido, Queen of Carthage* (1593). He recites the passage for the Players at 2.2.390 so as to jog their memory of it, beginning at that part of the narrative where Aeneas tells his new lover, Dido, about the fall of the city of Troy. This is a moment in *Hamlet* where the style shifts markedly from the plausibly naturalistic tenor of much of the rest of the play to pointed artifice. Some critics have claimed that Hamlet is not genuinely praising this arguably overblown, Marlovian dramatic idiom but, rather, merely satirizing it. The late seventeenth-century poet and playwright John Dryden, for example, grumbled about the 'blown puffy style' (Thompson and Taylor, 266) of this passage, which he believed to be a quotation from another Elizabethan playwright. More likely, it is the imitation of Marlowe's style. Shakespeare is arguably memorializing Marlowe who died in 1593 and whose passing he lamented in *As You Like It* when he referred to Marlowe (who was also an author of pastoral poetry) as the '[d]ead shepherd' (3.5.82). There is nothing in the play to suggest that Hamlet has any qualms about the quality of the versification of the speech he has memorized. On the contrary, Hamlet points out that the play from which he recites to the Players appealed only to discerning spectators, rather than to those who said 'there were no sallets in the lines to make the matter savoury' (2.2.379–80). In other words, there were spectators who did not appreciate the poetry and wanted something more spiced-up. What is important here is the idea that Shakespeare is truly attentive to the dramatic poetry of his time and that he has Hamlet show his admiration for a play – in this case Marlowe's *Dido* – that was less than popular with audiences.

Unlike the play-within-the-play, which is composed of rhymed pentameter couplets, Hamlet's speech to the Players is in blank verse. For all that, the verse definitively necessitates a departure from the more natural intonations that characterize the rest of the play's lines. The tone required leans toward the declamatory, although, of course, Hamlet famously warns the actors away from the pompous enunciation of dramatic verse. This might seem like a contradiction, but it isn't. Iambic pentameter was the form of verse nearest to the natural rhythms of spoken English, but its proximity to or distance from everyday speech could, nonetheless, still vary quite markedly:

> *The rugged Pyrrhus like th' Hyrcanian beast …*
> – 'Tis not so. It begins with Pyrrhus.
> *The rugged Pyrrhus, he whose sable arms,*
> *Black as his purpose, did the night resemble*
> *When he lay couched in th'ominous horse,*
> *Hath now this dread and black complexion smeared*
> *With heraldry more dismal, head to foot.*
> *Now is he total gules, horridly tricked*
> *With blood of fathers, mothers, daughters, sons,*
> *Baked and impasted with the parching streets*
> *That lend a tyrannous and a damned light*
> *To their lord's murder; roasted in wrath and fire,*
> *And thus o'ersized with coagulate gore,*
> *With eyes like carbuncles, the hellish Pyrrhus*
> *Old grandsire Priam seeks.*

(2.2.388–402)

In this passage Hamlet enacts both the frailty of memory as he tries to recollect the opening line, as well as its potency as he narrates the famous legend told by both Virgil and Ovid, and retold by Marlowe. This speech adroitly coincides with one of the themes of the play – the memory of dead fathers. Hamlet promised the Ghost that he would erase from his mind 'all trivial fond records' (1.5.99), but here he is able to recite a long passage about the Trojan War, some lines from which we examined in the previous chapter. However, the Greek Pyrrhus was also the avenging son of Achilles who enters Troy to enact his vengeance on its king, Priam, and his family. That first line, which Hamlet professes to have misremembered, associates revenge with savage, bestial killing since '*the Hyrcanian beast*' is a tiger. (Hyrcania was the name of a region near the Caspian Sea renowned for its tigers.) Initially, then, the avenging Pyrrhus is presented as an animal, bestial and inhuman.

Even with Hamlet's self-correction, Pyrrhus does not recover his humanity. He ceases to be a tiger only to become a black demon. His armour is black with its 'sable arms' and so is his 'complexion'. Devils were traditionally represented, both in art and on the stage, as black-faced. In this way, Pyrrhus resembles Hamlet, who also wears black in mourning for his father – his 'inky cloak' (like black ink), his 'customary suits of solemn black', his 'nighted colour' and his 'suit of woe' (1.2.77; 68; 78; 86). In all versions of the play, when Ophelia reminds him that his father has been dead for four months, he makes a sour joke about giving his mourning garments to the devil and wearing black fur himself. In doing so, he ostensibly makes a departure from his fully human identity to that of a beast:

'So long? Nay, then, let the devil wear black, for
I'll have a suit of sables!'

(3.2.122–3)

Arguably making the connection to the bestial much earlier in the play than in our edition, in Q1 Hamlet describes his cloak as 'sable' (dark fur) rather than 'inky', though it is more likely that there the fur is meant merely to denote Hamlet's royal status.

Shakespeare pauses in the speech to describe Pyrrhus' frame of mind, the nature of his intentions prior to taking action: '*he whose sable arms, / Black as his purpose, did the*

night resemble / When he lay couched in th'ominous horse'
(2.2.390–2). After Hamlet corrects his memory of the passage,
he moves from the instinctive, unthinking attack of a tiger to
the interval in which Pyrrhus had lain hidden in the wooden
horse. This enforced hiatus serves as a parallel to Hamlet's
delay – a period during which the avenging son is suspended
between intent and action. This is an ominous moment, too,
in the sense that it foreshadows Laertes' promise to revenge
his father.

Once he metamorphoses from tiger to demon, Pyrrhus'
transformation in this passage is almost complete. If Hamlet
feared in Act 1 that the Ghost's demand for revenge came
from hell, Pyrrhus offers evidence that it does in Act 2. There
is nothing heroic about Pyrrhus' revenge here, unlike Virgil's
version of the story, and there is only one moment in the play
when Hamlet identifies himself with such demonic vengeance.
This is Hamlet's vampire moment: 'Now could I drink hot
blood' (3.2.380), a practice in the early modern period
associated with witchcraft. Hamlet does not finally pledge
himself to hell, although Laertes does: 'To hell allegiance,
vows to the blackest devil' (4.5.130). The audience is at that
point in a position to compare the three avengers. Pyrrhus is
demonstrably the most terrifying of them.

Once he begins his killing spree, Pyrrhus' appearance becomes
even more horrific, departing from even the most ferocious
identities of the natural world. In the scorched, 'parching'
streets of burning Troy, he is now encrusted, *'Baked and
impasted'*, in the dried blood of those he has slaughtered. King
Hamlet was similarly crusted over by poison when murdered by
Claudius. Priam's murder will be illuminated with this *'damned
light'*, and Pyrrhus becomes not a noble warrior or honour-
bound avenging son, but rather a merciless, raging monster as
he seeks to kill an age-enfeebled grandfather. He is *'o'ersized'*
with congealed blood. '[O]'*ersized*' may mean that Pyrrhus
looks bigger because of the thick, baked-on blood stuck to his
body, but the word probably also refers to 'size' – a thick, sticky
primer used to prepare a surface before applying paint. Thus

the word returns us to Pyrrhus himself as a painted armorial design. Such an insignia derived from the medieval code of chivalric conduct when knights went into battle carrying shields decorated with armorial bearings. Despite having transformed into the type of image that might decorate a warrior's shield, Pyrrhus represents the antithesis of honourable combat that such chivalric ornament was meant to signify.

The layer of imagery in this passage pertaining to heraldry is especially significant because Shakespeare himself had successfully applied for a coat of arms, which was awarded in 1596. He did so on behalf of his father who, along with all his descendants, then acquired the status of gentlemen as opposed to being mere commoners. In 1568, Shakespeare's father had the design for his coat of arms drawn up or, to use the technical term, 'tricked' – just as Pyrrhus is *'tricked'* in blood. For reasons that are unclear, Shakespeare's father was unable to proceed with his application. Shakespeare's renewal of the application to the College of Arms on behalf of his father was not revenge, of course, but it was a way of reviving his father's claim for social advancement.

Shakespeare describes Pyrrhus' metamorphosis into a demonic armorial device in the very specific, technical lexicon of heraldry. Margreta de Grazia notes in *Hamlet Without Hamlet* that *'sable'*, *'tricked'*, *'gules'*, *'gore'* and *'carbuncles'* are all words used in heraldry and can be found in John Guillim's *A Display of Heraldrie* (1611) (de Grazia, 94). '[G]ore' and *'carbuncle'* refer to particular heraldic devices, while *'gules'*, the colour red, is, of course, a brighter hue than *'sable'* (black). But within this context, it is not paint but blood. This is *'dismal'* heraldry indeed, and while we use this word to mean something gloomy or cheerless, in Shakespeare's time 'dismal' carried more dire connotations. It meant disastrous or evil because it derived from the Latin *dies mali*, or days of ill omen, simultaneously harking back to and fulfilling the promise of *'th'ominous horse'* that destroys Troy. The final tragedy in *Hamlet* is later described in similar terms: 'The sight is dismal' (5.2.351).

Let us now compare the Pyrrhus passage in *Hamlet* with some of the lines from Marlowe's *Dido*:

AENEAS

> At last came Pirrhus fell and full of ire,
> His harnesse dropping bloud, and on his speare
> The mangled head of *Priams* yongest sonne,
> And after him his band of Mirmidons,
> With balles of wilde fire in their murdering pawes,
> Which made the funerall flame that burnt faire
> Troy.

(2.1.210–16)

It is important to be clear that the objective of this exercise is not to discover that Marlowe is an inferior versifier. Rather, it is to point out some similarities and differences between the two writers. Notice, for example, that the ends of the lines in *Dido* allow a clear pause for breath – they are **end-stopped** lines. We can also see how Shakespeare has followed Marlowe in that Pyrrhus' troops here are also fire-brandishing beasts whose 'murdering pawes', rather than human limbs and hands, clearly anticipate Shakespeare's demonic Pyrrhus. There are arresting images, too: 'The mangled head of *Priams* yongest sonne.' This line although it refers to a grown son, powerfully intimates a beheaded, defaced child, and Marlowe leaves to our imaginations the violently distorted and bloody features of its perhaps broken skull. In the heart-breaking, elegiac last line, the letter 'f' repeats in the first and last lines of the passage so that the alliterative pairs 'fell and full', together with the final 'funerall flame', work almost as a pattern of cause and consequence – fury breeds funerals.

Almost every line of Shakespeare's passage is much more complicated and dense, exhibiting what Thompson and Taylor refer to as 'the mesmeric intricacy of Shakespeare's language' (115). Take, for example, that extraordinary simile, 'eyes like carbuncles'. We might consider, too, the difference in meaning between Marlowe's Pirrhus who '[drops] bloud' and Shakespeare's Pyrrhus who is physically amplified with 'coagulate gore'. Do not, however, be tempted to dismiss Marlowe as the lesser talent. Not only was he Shakespeare's greatest rival, but he was also his exact contemporary (they were both born in 1564) as well as his greatest contemporary influence. Remember that Marlowe wrote *Dido* around 1593. Shakespeare was a much more experienced playwright by the time he wrote *Hamlet*. Had Marlowe not been murdered in his twenty-ninth year, he might even have surpassed Shakespeare in literary fame. Alas, we will never know.

Shakespeare's rhetorical techniques: Passage analysis (2.2.1–17)

The twentieth-century poet W. H. Auden, commenting on the maturation of Shakespeare's language, wrote that in *Hamlet*, 'Shakespeare is also developing a more flexible verse. He started off with the end-stopped Marlovian and lyric lines that were suitable to high passion. In *Hamlet* he experiments with the caesura, the stop in the middle of the line, to develop a middle voice, a voice neither passionate nor prosaic' (Auden, 160). Another technique used in the play is **enjambment**. This is essentially a run-on line where the phrase or sentence runs over onto the next line. It is a way of playing the pauses that occur in the natural rhythms of speech against the pause at the end of the line, which is where a break would seem logical. In an enjambed line, the end of the line does not coincide with a normal pause in speech, and if you stop for a breath, the line either won't make sense or it will sound very jagged. Consider when Claudius offers his rather formal greeting to Rosencrantz and Guildenstern:

> Welcome, dear Rosencrantz and Guildenstern.
> Moreover that we much did long to see you
> The need we have to use you did provoke

Our hasty sending. Something have you heard
Of Hamlet's transformation – so call it
Sith nor th'exterior nor the inward man
Resembles that it was. What it should be
More than his father's death, that thus hath put him
So much from th'understanding of himself
I cannot dream of. I entreat you both
That, being of so young days brought up with him
And sith so neighboured to his youth and haviour
That you vouchsafe your rest here in our Court
Some little time, so by your companies
To draw him on to pleasures and to gather
So much as from occasion you may glean,
Whether aught to us unknown afflicts him thus
That opened lies within our remedy.

(2.2.1–17)

In the first line of Claudius's greeting, the sentence fits perfectly within the line: it is an end-stopped line because the natural pause coincides perfectly with the end of the line. However, if you attempt to read the passage with pauses after 'provoke' at the end of line 3, or after 'heard' at the end of line 4; or after 'him' in line 8, or 'gather' in line 15, because the meaning of these lines bleeds into the next, you will find that the sense of the passage rapidly breaks down. This enjambment creates a much more naturalistic flow of speech in that it lessens the emphasis at the end of the line and loosens the hold of the metre even as the metre remains to undergird what is being said. Notice, too, that many of the significant pauses, or caesuras, in the above passage occur, as Auden remarked, in the middle of the lines. Shakespeare thus ensures that the verse does not draw undue attention to itself – it is not 'bragging' (Nashe and Jonson could have no complaints).

The stress patterns of this passage are also worthy of note. In the line, 'To draw him on to pleasures and to gather', the stress is on 'ga' rather than 'er', which creates an unstressed ending. Shakespeare also uses so-called **feminine endings** – lines with an extra, unstressed syllable, such as: 'And sith so neighboured to his youth and haviour,' which highlights the recurrent vowel sounds, the assonance (repetition of the same vowel sounds in proximate words) of 'neighb**ou**red', 'y**ou**th', and '[be]hav**iou**r'. The expression 'youth and 'haviour' (meaning youthful behaviour) is also an instance of a specific rhetorical figure known as **hendiadys** that is prominent in *Hamlet*. Hendiadys literally means 'one through two' and refers to instances in which two words are joined by a conjunction to express a single, complex idea and where typically one of the words modifies the other. Thus, the noun, 'youth' modifies another noun, 'haviour' where we would normally expect the adjective 'youthful', as in 'youthful behaviour'.

Now that we have identified these techniques, how can we use them to understand more fully what is going on at this point in the play? These lines occur in the passage where Claudius welcomes Rosencrantz and Guildenstern to the court in Elsinore. Claudius wants them to glean information from Hamlet, but he does not come the heavy here insisting or demanding that they interrogate his nephew. This line, with its soft ending and its rationale for setting the pair to spy on Hamlet, conveys avuncular concern – Rosencrantz, Guildenstern and Hamlet are close to one another in age and in manners. While the meaning of Claudius' 'youth and haviour' is clear, the rhetorical doubling up here reminds us, Claudius' assertion to the contrary, that Rosencrantz and Guildenstern are, in fact, nothing like Hamlet and if they were, they would not be so eager to spy on him.

The key point to bear in mind is that all these different techniques – especially, perhaps, the discernable patterns of repetition and recurrence in the play – serve to render its language more subtle and sophisticated, as opposed to crude, obtrusive linguistic arrangements penned with 'the swelling bombast of bragging blank verse'. While such techniques are not unique to Shakespeare, his supreme mastery of them makes his dramatic verse more flexible and closer to actual speech than the kind of verse parodied by Nashe.

Rhyme and lyricism

Because unrhymed blank verse, the form of dramatic poetry that Shakespeare used the most, is flexible enough to sound natural, when Shakespeare wanted to emphasize something or draw attention to the artifice of poetic language, he incorporated rhyme. For example, at the end of a scene, Shakespeare often uses capping couplets:

> The time is out of joint; O cursed spite
> That ever I was born to set it right!

> (1.5.186–7)

The play-within-the-play is entirely in rhyme and encourages the audience to reflect on the artifice of theatre itself. Conversely, Shakespeare sometimes uses heightened lyrical language while remaining within the framework of end-stopped blank verse. For example, Horatio alerts his companions of the night's watch to daybreak:

> But look, the morn in russet mantle clad
> Walks o'er the dew of yon high eastward hill.

> (1.1.165–6)

The morning is presented here in figurative rather than literal language – as someone wearing a red-brown coat made of the sort of coarse cloth worn by a country person, and he seems to be taking a gentle amble over the hills. We never speak like this in daily life. This is speech that is deliberately lyrical, using the **trope** of personification. A trope is any literary or rhetorical device that removes language from its most literal meaning. It is indeed this gap between the literal and the literary – the bald fact of something and its more nuanced, more imaginative representation – that literary works are required to traverse.

You might wonder why Shakespeare did not use the prosaic form of expression, 'Look, first light.' It becomes immediately obvious once you think about it, however, that this is a less poetic expression and one which would hardly be appropriate to describe the relief of dawn after a night which has witnessed the apparition of a Ghost who has walked, not with the natural rhythm of an early morning stroll, but '[w]ith martial stalk' (1.1.65). The description of the Ghost's walk alerts the nervous system:

MARCELLUS
     Thus twice before, and jump at this dead hour,
     With martial stalk hath he gone by our watch.

                              (1.1.64–5)

The staccato rhythm of the first line contrasts with the stilted pace of the second, the 'martial stalk' that characterizes the stiff and angry, militaristic gait of the Ghost's nightly perambulations. The contrast between 'jump' and 'dead' also neatly conveys the shock of the apparition. '[J]ump' here means just or exactly at this time – at midnight – but even in early modern English, 'jump' expressed its modern sense which, in this context, would be the natural reaction to seeing a ghost – it would make you start. The 'dead hour' is the hour at which the dead walk, 'In the dead waste and middle of the night' (1.2.197). Both 'dead' and 'jump' refer to a precise moment, namely the time the Ghost appeared, but these words also suggest the dreaded terror of the apparition and the fear of sudden death. Horatio uses the word 'jump' again at the end of the play to mean 'immediately after' during his exchange with the Ambassador: 'But, since so jump upon this bloody question' (5.2.359). '[J]ump' thus conveys abrupt, even decisive action in a play characterized by deferral and delay, and it carries connotations of leaping (Macbeth hopes to 'jump the life to come' [1.7.7]), while 'dead' has invariably ominous overtones. In contrast to the stalking and jumping in the first account of how the Ghost appears, Horatio's benign description of the 'russet morn' seems to belong to a different genre – lyrical poetry – to the aubade, the song of the dawn, not to revenge tragedy. It is the juxtaposition between the lyrical beginning of the day and the passing of the terrors of night that temporarily dissipates suspense, only to build it up again when Hamlet himself witnesses the Ghost.

Prose madness

Shakespeare often transmutes the diction of common life to remarkable dramatic effect. Hamlet entreats the Ghost, 'If thou hast any sound or use of voice, / Speak to me' (1.1.127–8). 'Speak to me' is a direct message, whereas 'sound' and 'voice' expand the command they preface into the language of lyricism. This occurs in a verse passage, but Shakespeare has another strategy for traversing the terrain between ordinary language and poetic language, and that is prose.

As we saw in Chapter One, the Renaissance derived its precepts for tragedy from Aristotle's *Poetics*. Aristotle associated tragedy with high and lofty matters and aristocratic persons, while he associated comedy with the ordinary and everyday and with the lowborn. These distinctions made sense within the context of the rigidly hierarchized society of ancient Greece, and Shakespeare inherited them. Blank verse is generally the form of language given to aristocratic characters, whereas lower-class characters tend to speak in prose, in part reflecting the different ways of speaking across the social order prior to the advent of modern democracy. Importantly, these are conventions about dramatic speech, not ironclad rules, and there are moments in Shakespeare – though not in *Hamlet* – when lower-class characters speak in verse. The prose passages in *Hamlet* follow classical conventions so that, for example, when Hamlet addresses the gravediggers or the players, he speaks in prose. However, prose is no more without artifice than verse. Nor was prose always used because it was supposed to be more life-like; rather, it was used strategically to define very specific dramatic situations.

Consider, for example, when Hamlet gives acting instructions to the players:

> Speak the speech, I pray you, as I pronounced
> it to you – trippingly on the tongue. But if you mouth
> it as many of our players do, I had as lief the town-crier
> spoke my lines. Nor do not saw the air too much with
> your hand, thus, but use all gently; for, in the very
> torrent, tempest and, as I may say, whirlwind of your
> passion, you must acquire and beget a temperance that
> may give it smoothness. O, it offends me to the soul to
> hear a robustious periwig-pated fellow tear a passion to
> tatters, to very rags, to split the ears of the groundlings,
> who for the most part are capable of nothing but
> inexplicable dumb-shows and noise. I would have such
> a fellow whipped for o'erdoing Termagant – it out-
> Herods Herod. Pray you avoid it.
>
>   (3.2.1–14).

What makes this passage prose is that it does not have the regular, recurring patterns of pause (measure) and stress (metre) that characterize verse. The actor now decides where to pause and place stress. There are, however, still-discernible patterns in this passage, such as the energetically alliterative 'torrent', 'tempest', 'tatters' and 'Termagant', used to echo 'trippingly'. Hamlet's prose style is that of rhythmic, mellifluous speech, of which 'trippingly on the tongue' is a perfect example. This passage is also replete with vivid imagery, and Hamlet's prose brings some characters – bad actors all – vividly to life: the town crier who shouts out proclamations issued by the Crown; the 'robustious periwig-pated fellow' whose histrionics shred and destroy language; and two other characters particularly susceptible to over-the-top, bad acting. These are Termagant, the deity Elizabethans believed Muslims to have worshipped, and the biblical figure King Herod of Judea. After the three kings from the east brought news of the birth of the messiah in Bethlehem, Herod ordered the massacre of all male children aged less than two years old. As the most famous baby killer in history, Herod was presented in medieval mystery play cycles as a ranting tyrant. Since such plays were devised prior to the advent of professional acting companies, the temptation to overplay such a role was probably not much resisted.

In *Hamlet*, the opening of Act 5 is a shift into the prose world-view of the lowly, joke-cracking Gravediggers who daily confront death but who are, unlike Hamlet, far from paralysed by its gaping jaws. Instead, they toss skeletons about in such jocular fashion that Hamlet wonders if their labour inures them to the predicament of mortality, which ultimately and inexorably confronts all human beings. However, the language of the Gravediggers, while in the prose appropriate to their social position as lowborn, manual labourers, is far from superficial. Indeed, the powers of reasoning demonstrated and parodied by the Gravedigger rival those of even the play's tragic hero: 'If the man go to this water and drown himself, it is, willy-nilly, he goes. Mark you that. But if the water come to him and drown him, he drowns not himself' (5.1.16–19). The Gravedigger's is as profound a meditation on the mysteries of death and volition as anything in Hamlet's soliloquies. However, the Gravedigger resists getting to the point, or what his fellow delver calls 'the truth on't' (5.1.23). While elevated language may be an avenue to truth, comedy arrives there by circuitous means. As Rebecca Bushnell points out, 'Both the "low" and the "high" have ... always been a part of the language of tragedy, for in tragedy words are understood both as a shield from the truth as well as the means to it' (Bushnell, 50). Thus, for example, Ophelia's primary identity in Act 5 is that of someone who commits suicide, which is to say that the fact of her self-slaughter overwhelms even her gendered identity so that she is, as the Gravedigger says, neither man nor woman: 'One that was a woman, sir, but rest her soul she's dead' (5.1.127–8).

Another literary convention in drama of the period is that letters are written in prose. An example is Hamlet's letter to Horatio in Act 4 scene 6 explaining how he escaped from the ship bound for England. Apart from the obvious fact that a verse letter might seem implausible by any estimation, there is a good theatrical reason for prose here. Prose allows the character reading the letter onstage to differentiate clearly his or her language from that of the sender of the letter. Letters are important to the progression of the plot, and it is vitally important that the audience understands the play's action clearly. We can hear Hamlet's voice in the letter, his complex way of accessing reality:

> *They have dealt with*
> *me like thieves of mercy, but they knew what they did*
> (4.6.19–20).

These lines contain two enigmatically distorted echoes of episodes from Christ's crucifixion. The first is when the 'good thief' being crucified with Jesus is shown mercy, and the second is when Jesus says of his tormentors, 'Father, forgive them; for they know not what they do' (Lk. 23.34). Though it is clear that the pirates allowed Hamlet to live for motives of their own, this remains a cryptic, rather than full, account of what happened aboard the pirate ship.

The prose speeches most important to the central themes of the play are those where Hamlet is either mad or pretending to be mad. Because it constitutes a form of disordered speech that is ostensibly inimical to the measured language of blank verse, madness – whether pretended or real – is typically in prose. When the mad or ostensibly mad depart from prose they typically resort not to iambic pentameter but to song. Ophelia's intensely lyrical madness manifests, of course, primarily in song. Even Hamlet, during one of his mad fits, takes a line from a ballad about the biblical figure Jephthah, and we can tell that this is the case because the line is in ballad metre with seven stresses and fourteen syllables, commonly known as a fourteener and more formally termed iambic heptameter. The line is therefore a marked departure from the five stresses and ten syllables that characterize the pentameter line, and its metre, typical of ballads of the period, was considered old-fashioned by the time Shakespeare was writing:

> O Jephthah, judge of Israel, what a treasure hadst
> thou?

> (2.2.339–40)

However, from a technical point of view, prose only denotes insanity where Hamlet's language clearly deviates from rational coherence. Thus, for example, 'mad speeches', such as his question to Polonius, 'Do you see yonder cloud that's almost in shape of a camel?' (3.2.367–8), are in prose. In other instances, even when those around him question his sanity, if Hamlet's language is completely rational, he speaks in verse. For example, when his incontrovertibly lucid rhetoric cleaves his mother's heart in two in Act 3 scene 4, he speaks in verse. This is so despite the fact that he sees the Ghost his mother cannot see and that she believes to be the product of Hamlet's insanity: 'This is the very coinage of your brain' (3.4.135). Similarly, at Ophelia's graveside, where both Claudius and Gertrude assert that he is mad, Hamlet's again incontestably logical speech is in blank verse (see 5.1.263–73). Gertrude is arguably trying to protect her son from Laertes' rage when she says, 'This is mere madness' (5.1.273), but in any case, when Hamlet angrily attacks Laertes, the audience may feel that he has finally come to his senses. Indeed, one of the arguments in favour of the idea that Hamlet is not really mad is that he tells us so in blank verse: 'That I essentially am not in madness / But mad in craft' (3.4.185–6). Since people who are out of their wits sometimes insist that they are sane, had he made this assertion in prose, we would do well to question it. Whether or not we believe him to be mad, however, it remains the case that whenever Hamlet's language veers away from rational coherence, Shakespeare has him speak in prose rather than blank verse.

In Hamlet's exchange with Polonius in Act 2, there is a strong sense that Hamlet's madness is arguably too acute to be genuine rather than contrived. The obtuse Polonius is not aware of it, but his commentary nonetheless serves to guide the audience toward such an interpretation:

> POLONIUS
> — Will you walk out of the air, my lord?
> HAMLET   Into my grave.
> POLONIUS   [*aside*]   Indeed, that's out of the air.
> How pregnant sometimes his replies are – a happiness
> that often madness hits on, which reason and sanity
> could not so prosperously be delivered of.
>
> (2.2.203–8)

Hamlet's irrational prose is clever, witty. His riposte here is terse and lightning quick. As Polonius remarks in the aside we noted earlier, 'Though this be madness, yet there is / method in't' (2.2.202–3). What is genuine here, as we know from the first soliloquy, is Hamlet's inclination towards suicide – the urge to walk into his grave, which comports with the melancholy demeanour Ophelia described in the previous scene, when Hamlet arrived at her 'closet' (2.1.74) in emotional and sartorial disarray. For all that, neither his 'love melancholy' nor his suicidal propensities rob him completely of his powers of reason, at least not at this stage of the play.

This is not so clearly the case in Act 3 when Hamlet's dejection has transformed into rage against the women in his life:

> HAMLET   O God, your only jig-maker! What should
> a man do but be merry, for look you how cheerfully my
> mother looks, and my father died within's two hours!
>
> (3.2.118–20)

Hamlet is like the proverbial lunatic who does not know what day of the week it is. He seems to have lost all sense of time when he abbreviates the period since his father's death to a mere two hours. He also takes on the role of comedian, the 'jig-maker', with the self-deprecating, self-consciousness of someone who is watching his life from a distance, rather than fully immersed in living it. What he says, however, is simultaneously mad and completely astute – as well as poisonously bitter – about his mother's almost instant recovery from his father's death.

There are also, however, prose speeches where Hamlet is not just conspicuously lucid but also deeply philosophical, and where prose draws attention precisely to this distinctive register of thought. For example, when Hamlet accepts the invitation to what Horatio fears will be imminent death in the form of the fencing contest with Laertes, he utters what have become some of the play's most oft-quoted lines:

> There is special
> providence in the fall of a sparrow. If it be, 'tis not to
> come. If it be not to come, it will be now. If it be not
> now, yet it will come. The readiness is all ...

> (5.2.197–200)

This speech revisits the language of Hamlet's first soliloquy, 'To be or not to be,' and glances at the doctrine of predestination. According to this much-debated doctrine, God had already preordained the course of human affairs, almost to the point where the will and the actions of human beings were completely cancelled out. When Hamlet famously opines, '[T]his goodly frame the earth seems / to me a sterile promontory' (2.2.264–5), and that man is 'the paragon of animals' (2.2.273), he also speaks in prose:

> this most excellent canopy
> the air, look you, this brave o'erhanging firmament, this

majestical roof fretted with golden fire, why it
appeareth nothing to me but a foul and pestilent
congregation of vapours. What piece of work is a man …

(2.2.265–9)

For all that this famous **apostrophe** (an abstract address to a
sometimes-absent third party) expresses profound melancholy,
the speech also epitomizes rational thinking and deploys an
ornate, highly figurative, lyrical vocabulary to stress with
impressive elocutionary force the antithesis between the
beauty of life and Hamlet's abjection.

Thomas Nashe

It might be tempting to think that because he was so unique,
Shakespeare did not emulate other writers. As we have already
seen in relation to Marlowe, this was not the case. However,
Shakespeare's language – and not only or even primarily his
poetry – was also very much influenced by one of his contemporaries who wrote mainly in prose, Thomas Nashe.

J. J. M. Tobin argues that Shakespeare 'steeped himself in
the works of Nashe so thoroughly that words, phrases, themes,
and cadences recur in his own works, sometimes as a result
of subconscious association, sometimes by calculation' (388).
The redheaded, university-educated Thomas Nashe (one of the
'university wits', unlike Shakespeare, who had only a grammar
school education) was a prose writer known for his linguistic brio
and his daring and extraordinarily ingenious verbal acrobatics.
It is important to keep in mind, then, that Shakespeare was not
an isolated genius, but a writer participating fully in the cultural
life of literary London. His contemporaries were some of the
most adept writers not only of their own age but also of any
period of writing in the English language.

For instance, the idea presented early on in *Hamlet* that
the Danes are drunken swine comes from Nashe. Moreover,

Shakespeare is indebted to Nashe not just for the idea but, even more importantly, also for the language in which it is expressed. 'The heavy-headed gluttonous house dove' (1.210) and 'this surly swinish generation' (1.180) are not quotations from *Hamlet*, but from Nashe's *Pierce Penniless His Supplication to the Devil* (1592) (Thompson and Taylor, 72). Consider the parallel passage from *Hamlet*:

HAMLET
 The King doth wake tonight and takes his rouse,
 Keeps wassail and the swaggering upspring reels,
 And as he drains his draughts of Rhenish down
 The kettledrum and trumpet thus bray out
 The triumph of his pledge.
HORATIO   Is it a custom?
HAMLET
 Ay, marry is't,
 But to my mind, though I am native here
 And to the manner born, it is a custom
 More honoured in the breach than the observance.
 This heavy-headed revel east and west
 Makes us traduced and taxed of other nations:
 They clepe us drunkards and with swinish phrase
 Soil our addition ...

            (1.4.8–20)

The Danes were the renowned inebriates of early modern Europe. When the English ambassador visited Copenhagen, Sir William Segar, Garter King-at-Arms, wrote in his notebook on 14 July, 1603: '[I]t would make a man sick to hear of their drunken healths [toasts]: use hath brought it into a fashion, and fashion made it a habit, which ill beseems our nation to imitate' (Raleigh, Lee, and Onions, 17). Shakespeare's lines literally mean that there's a loud, drunken party at the court and that these disorderly rituals have tarnished the reputation of the Danes. This carousing is accompanied not by music but by the bestial braying of 'kettledrum and trumpet'. Hamlet tells us other nations call them drunken pigs: 'They clepe us drunkards and with swinish phrase / Soil our addition [good name].' 'Soil' suggests the dirt associated with swine – pig shit, an idea that is echoed when Hamlet calls Claudius' and Gertrude's bed a 'nasty sty' (3.4.92). The recurrent vowel sounds in 'This heavy-headed revel east and west' creates a dizzying effect that begins with the alliterative 'heavy-headed' and moves horizontally across the line, zig-zagging 'east and west', which figuratively creates the sensation of drunkenness. The lines, 'Keeps wassail and the swaggering upspring reels / And as he drains his draughts of Rhenish down' also have a vertiginous effect: 'upspring' and 'down'. The suggestion is that keeping wassail – that is, drinking numerous toasts – leads to riotous dancing, or 'reels', but also reeling drunkenness. The sudden descent from 'upspring' is more fully emphasized because of the alliteration in the phrase 'drains his draughts', along with the internal rhyme of 'wassail' (toasts) and 'swaggering' as well as the double vowels in 'keeps' and 'reels'. A great deal of unsteady movement is conveyed in these lines. However, the passage is often cut from performance and, indeed, does not appear in the 1623 Folio text of the play. Because James I's queen was Danish (Anne of Denmark), it used to be thought that these lines were omitted so as not to offend the monarch. Modern editors, however, tend towards the view that the lines slow down the action of the play and that Shakespeare's point in including them was to emphasize Hamlet's preoccupation with his stepfather's vices. However, from the point of view of Shakespeare as a writer, what is particularly interesting about this passage is that he not only worked into *Hamlet* ideas from other authors, both ancient and modern, but also that he included some of the *language* of his contemporaries in the play.

Rhetoric

The *Oxford English Dictionary* defines eloquence as fluent, intensely expressive, forceful, and persuasive language, and as Richard A. Lanham points out, *Hamlet* is haunted by it (129–43). In many respects, this reflects a historically specific phenomenon. Elizabethan humanists, those who looked back to the ancient world as a model for reshaping the present, shaking it from its medieval past, understood not only that language could carry and contain powerful messages, acting as a delivery system, but also that language could itself constitute a form of power. Thus, language did not always need to be backed up by, say, violence (sending an army) or diplomacy (sending an ambassador) because it could actually be violent or diplomatic. The distinction is both critical and complex. The strategies Elizabethans used to elevate ordinary language and endow it with power were those of classical rhetoric. In his influential treatise *The Garden of Eloquence* (printed in both 1577 and 1594), Henry Peacham emphasized 'the secret and mighty power of perswuasion' (Peltonen, 15) as the predominant feature of the *ars rhetorica*, the 'art' of linguistic eloquence. Rhetoric was so powerful that it might make listeners do things not only against their inclinations, but also against their wills. Indeed, potent rhetoric could both lead and mislead those who heard it. The rules of rhetoric and the means of mastering them derived from the ancient world in which the *ars rhetorica* originated as a way of arguing persuasively for one's case in civic life. The Roman orator, Cicero, in *De Oratore*, exemplified rhetorical power and was particularly influential on early modern authors. An education in classical languages and the rhetorical prowess that accompanied them was thought to be appropriate preparation for a legal, clerical or ecclesiastical position in Elizabethan England. Rhetoric itself described a formal, systematized approach to powerful speech and writing. Training in rhetoric disciplined writers and instilled in them specific strategies of language.

Such training became second nature and enabled those thus trained in the arts of eloquence to put pen to paper on all kinds of occasions and in all states of feeling. Shakespeare's own rhetorical training in the Stratford grammar school honed his capacity to write to order for both patron and playhouse and thereby shaped his professional identity.

A key dimension of this training in eloquence involved speaking as well as writing in Latin. Even though by the sixteenth century it was not a spoken language anywhere in Europe, pupils were trained to declaim Cicero's speeches, and, like Polonius at the university, to act in Latin plays and to write in both Latin prose and verse. Lanham provides a useful description of the kind of rhetorical education in which Shakespeare had been drilled:

> Start your student young. Teach him a minute concentration on the word, how to write it, speak it, remember it. Stress memory in a massive, almost brutalizing way, develop it far in advance of conceptual understanding. Let words come first as objects and sounds long before they can, for a child, take on full meaning. They are looked *at* before they can be looked through. From the beginning, stress behavior as performance, reading aloud, speaking with gesture, a full range of histrionic adornment. Require no original thought. Demand instead an agile marshaling of the proverbial wisdom on any issue. Categorize this wisdom into predigested units, commonplaces, *topoi*. Dwell on their decorous fit into situation (Lanham, 2).

Laertes, who has been at university in Paris, clearly possesses education in these arts, though his execution of them is sometimes trite. His speech to Ophelia about protecting her virginity from Hamlet is almost parodic. There is certainly nothing original in the platitudes he rehearses: 'The chariest maid is prodigal enough / If she unmask her beauty to the moon' (1.3.35–6). Laertes' statement is almost risible. Even a court lady who removes her mask at night, or potentially even a woman who undresses by moonlight, is sufficiently promiscuous. This is followed by the old chestnut about how potential is blighted like a bud that never comes to blossom: 'The canker galls the infants of the spring / Too oft before their buttons be disclosed, / And in the morn and liquid dew of youth / Contagious blastments are most imminent' (1.3.38–41). This is repetition from memory – not spontaneous invention. Laertes, however, comes to see the limitations of formal rhetorical style when his sister descends into her exquisitely lyrical madness: Ophelia becomes eloquent. However, hers is not the eloquence of formal rhetorical training, but that of an imagination unleashed from the strictures both of rationality and of the social codes enforced upon women, and when Laertes describes its force, he utters some of the most moving lines given to him in the play:

> Hadst thou thy wits and didst persuade revenge
> It could not move thus.

> (4.5.163–4).

Not all eloquence, then, is a product of formal rhetoric, and despite being the crucial link between language and action, words and deeds, nor is all persuasive speech. Effective speech in any form, however, has real-world consequences, and Laertes interprets his sister's ditties as unsurpassably beautiful arguments for revenge.

Rhetorical terms

We have already looked at some rhetorical terms, like **ananta-clasis** (repeating a word but with a different meaning). Rhetorical devices such as this one were used to power up language. George Puttenham's *The Arte of English Poesie* (1589) made Latin and Greek rhetorical terms and literary figures available to readers in English. Shakespeare, equipped with his grammar-school training, used many of them. Rhetorical terms often have names that sound alarmingly medical: 'Yes, that rash looks like a nasty case of anadiplosis' (which we will discuss shortly). Learning something about these devices is not designed to turn you into a kind of literary train-spotter: 'Oh, look, there's anaphora!' **Anaphora** comes from a Greek word meaning to carry back and signals the repetition of a word at the start of successive phrases or lines – e.g. 'to die: to sleep – / To sleep, perchance to dream' (3.1.63–4). Fortunately, it is much more important to recognize a pattern and discern its effects than to remember what it is called. While it is sometimes very helpful to recognize these devices when you come across them, and indeed, they can be very handy to have on your critical tool belt, the point is not to simply name them; rather, it is important to see what kind of effect Shakespeare was working toward when he chose to use language in a particular way and to grasp the importance of how being aware of these techniques can assist your own inter-pretation of particular words, phrases or lines and of the play's broader themes. Thus, our investigation of how Shakespeare uses various rhetorical strategies of repetition helps us to see what the play is driving at. For example, 'to die: to sleep – / To sleep, perchance to dream' contains a list of verbs, all of which gesture to states beyond conscious awareness. The lulling effect of the anaphoric repetition of 'to sleep' conveys the sense of reprieve that Hamlet imagines as the departure from the painful condition of conscious awareness.

You are probably familiar with some rhetorical terms already, such as **alliteration**, which is the repetition of a letter or a sound at the beginning of words in close proximity to one another. For example, hoping to contain Hamlet and the threat he poses, Claudius orders Rosencrantz and Guildenstern to ship him off to England:

Arm you, I pray you, to this speedy voyage
For we will fetters put about this fear
Which now goes too free-footed.

(3.3.24–6)

Those five alliterative 'fs' around that central word 'fetters' work to bind this quasi-personified fear that has been danger-ously at large, and that final alliterative 'free-footed', although it means something like 'footloose', ironically puts the double lock on it.

Shakespeare also deploys the rhetorical strategy of allit-eration, for instance, when the Ghost describes how Claudius has used the persuasive power of rhetoric on Gertrude:

> Ay, that incestuous, that adulterate beast,
> With witchcraft of his wits, with traitorous gifts –
> O wicked wit and gifts that have the power
> So to seduce – won to his shameful lust
> The will of my most seeming-virtuous Queen.

> (1.5.42–6)

The alliterative 'w' sound in these lines culminates in Gertrude's 'will', both in the general sense of her agency and self-determination and in the sense of her sexual desire, represented in this passage by those insistent and often (though not always) alliterative 's' sounds. Notice, too, that the alliterative consonants 'w' and 's' are also repeated within two key words that end lines 43 and 44: 'lust' and 'power'. These words forcefully remind us of the nature of the moral problem here, but the repetition of the same conso-nants used in the instances of alliteration gets the message across all the more. Shamefully, not only has Gertrude been seduced by Claudius' 'wit' – his ingenuity and intellectual abilities – she has literally been bought off with his 'gifts'. Since the word 'gifts' is pointedly repeated, whether these are actual presents or Claudius' innate, personal talents remains ambiguous.

Anadiplosis, also known as **antistrophe,** is the repetition of the last word of one phrase or line to begin the next. When the Gravedigger uses this rhetorical figure, he turns expectations about language and class on their head:

It must be *se offendendo*. It cannot be else.
For here lies the point: if I drown myself wittingly, it
argues an **act**, and an **act** hath three branches – it is to
act, to do, to perform. Argal, she drowned herself
wittingly.

(5.1.9–13)

The Gravedigger is parodying exercises within the discipline
of logic as well as the processes of legal reasoning that belong
to his social superiors. [S]e *offendendo* means 'so offended',
but this could also possibly be the Gravedigger's mistake for *se
defendendo*, Latin for 'in self-defence'. 'Argal' is a corruption
of *ergo*, meaning 'thus' or 'for that reason', and was often
used as the final clause in a chain of logical argument.

Another fascinating aspect of these lines is that they
exemplify the way that language is always embedded in its
particular historical moment. This is especially evident here
because Shakespeare was alluding to the notorious case of
the 1554 suicide of the lawyer Sir James Hales who drowned
himself in a shallow stream at Thanington, near Canterbury.
Sir James had been unjustly imprisoned for refusing to bend
the law to the will of Queen Mary Tudor's government and
went mad as a result of his confinement. This was his second
suicide attempt – he had previously slit his wrists with a
penknife. His case went to court. Because suicide was a felony,
whatever property the person who committed suicide had
owned could be forfeited to the Crown, potentially leaving his
survivors homeless and penniless. The Hales' case provoked
a bizarre argument in court about whether the felony itself
was alleged to have occurred during Hales' lifetime or after
it: did he break the law while dead or alive? If he was dead
when the alleged felony occurred, then obviously no felony
had been committed. The legal reasoning that was presented
in court is the same as that used by the Gravedigger, namely
that the act of suicide can be divided into three parts: first,
imagining the deed; second, resolving to do it; and finally, the

actual execution of the imagined and resolved course of self-destruction. Hales' widow lost her suit, but the case remained an example of the potential absurdities of convoluted legal reasoning.

Another rhetorical feature very much associated with Shakespeare's tragedies is the tendency, as Simon Palfrey puts it, 'to use two words when one might do' (39). There are many, many examples of this in the play, and we have already considered the figure of hendiadys in which two words are joined by a conjunction even though one modifies the other. Shakespeare also uses **double epithets** where two words of the same or almost identical meaning are joined by a conjunction and **double adjectives** (pairs of adjectives). W. H. Auden noted this phenomenon of multiplying words as distinctive and argued that in *Hamlet*, it was a new phenomenon in Shakespeare's writing:

> *Hamlet* also shows a development in Shakespeare's use of the double adjective. From such a phrase as 'sweet and honey'd sentences' in *Henry V* (1.1.50), which is tautological, he moves to pairs of adjectives in *Hamlet* that combine the abstract and the concrete: Laertes' 'And keep you in the rear of your affection / Out of the **shot and danger** of desire [1.3.33–4] (Auden, 160).

Again, the main point is to look for Shakespeare's word patterns and to consider what effect he uses them to create. In 'the heat and flame of thy distemper' (3.4.119), we are almost burned by the phrase, while the phrase 'the brooch, indeed, / And gem of all the nation' (4.7.91–2) creates a mental picture of the bejewelled prince who is himself an ornament to his country. This lavish profusion of adjectives and nouns rounds out our understanding of a character or a situation as, for example, when Hamlet describes Fortinbras as the 'delicate and tender prince' (4.4.47), emphasizing his refinement, fastidiousness and fragility (a good idea, since Fortinbras is about to take over Denmark in the next Act). '[A] loving and a fair reply' (1.2.121) conveys the degree of courteousness expressed, while 'a puffed and reckless libertine' (1.3.48) gives the sense of inflated, careless behaviour. We have already mentioned 'wild and whirling words' (1.5.132), which Shakespeare used when he could have written 'wildly whirling words' or just 'wild words'. There are many more: the terrifying 'ponderous and marble jaws' (1.4.50) make us pause in horror as we work our way through the three syllables of that first word 'ponderous' before being confronted by the monumental solidity of those 'jaws'.

All of these figures constitute modes of repetition and amplification. They intensify and give density to meaning by complicating it and, at times, pushing the envelope in terms of its coherence. George T. Wright, who has also argued for the prevalence of these phenomena, especially in terms of the figure of hendiadys in *Hamlet*, observes that in such instances there is also 'sometimes a muddling of meanings, a deliberate violation of clear sense that is in perfect keeping with Shakespeare's exploration, in this period, of "things supernatural and causeless" (*All's Well That Ends Well*, 2.3.3)' (Wright, 12). For the audience, such carefully honed language registers as memorable phrases and images, providing the playgoer's imagination with a third and even a fourth dimension to what can be seen on stage.

Rhetoric, then, is essentially the art of eloquence – how to enhance the power of persuasion in language not just to make someone do something they would not normally want to do, but also to make them feel something (happy, sad, motivated, sympathetic) as they hear or read, as well as to encourage them to think in ways that are complex and at times even confusing. All of this is vital to Shakespeare's capacity to use language to shape his audience's response to the play.

Hamlet without words: 'The rest is silence' (5.2.342)

Poetic language is about sound, even if we are only sounding out the words in our heads. Shakespeare, of course, also wrote dramatic poetry to be vocalized by his actors so that the sound of words also works to organize their meaning. Hamlet's final words are some of the most profoundly philosophical in the play. What they mean and why they are so dramatically effective is best grasped by considering them, as we will do in this section, within the context of the play as a whole.

Earlier in the play, death is vividly associated with marble jaws and rotting cadavers that are a diet for worms. In other words, death has hitherto been figured as material content – skulls, dirt, graves and funeral monuments. In Hamlet's last line, however, death becomes entirely devoid of content or substance, denoting all that is beyond utterance, beyond language itself. Hamlet's silence offers a sharp contrast with the eerie sounds emanating from the Roman dead described by Horatio in Act 1. Perhaps this is because unlike Hamlet these are the rather more disturbing undead:

> A little ere the mightiest Julius fell
> The graves stood tenantless and the sheeted dead
> Did squeak and gibber in the Roman streets ...

> (1.1.113–15)

These Roman zombies are incapable of articulate pronouncement as the onomatopoeic 'squeak and gibber' suggests. They can say nothing, but the language with which Horatio describes them speaks volumes: the assonance of 'sheeted' and 'streets' and the rhetorical distinction between 'little' and 'mighty' and falling and standing ('Julius fell' and 'graves stood tenantless'). The double consonants of 'tenantless' and 'gibber' also mirror one another on the page to create a visually disturbing undercurrent to the passage.

The four, short monosyllabic words in the first line contrast sharply with the elongated effects of the hissing, sibilant 's' sounds of 'mightiest Julius'. The repeated consonant 'd' at the end of 'sheeted' and at the beginning and end of 'dead' also works to insist that, despite their chatter, these shroud-covered figures are indeed actually dead. The sound of the lines thus provides an ominous undercurrent that exceeds any attempt to paraphrase their meaning. The dead should be silent, and that they are not is what is so unnerving.

Squeaking and gibbering conveys nothing of the monumental dignity of death that is associated with Hamlet's father, whose 'canonized bones' have been 'hearsed in death' (1.4.47). These mortal remains have been made holy and placed appropriately in the sepulchre. However, the mourning rites due to him have been savagely curtailed by his widow's hurried remarriage. This resonates with one of the key themes of classical tragedy. In Sophocles' *Antigone*, Antigone seeks a proper burial for her brother whose rites of mourning and burial have been denied. Polonius, too, has suffered truncated burial rights, as Claudius admits: '[W]e have done but greenly / In hugger-mugger to inter him' (4.5.83–4). That wonderful expression 'hugger-mugger' contains another echo of death among the ancient Romans: Thomas North's translation of Plutarch's account of Julius Caesar refers to the fact that Antonius wished the murdered Caesar's body to be 'honorably buried and not in hugger mugger' (Thompson and Taylor, 380). Since Shakespeare had probably just written *Julius Caesar* when he composed *Hamlet*, North's translation of Plutarch's *Lives* was a book he had very recently consulted. It is also interesting that those 'ug' sounds in 'hugger mugger' echo Hamlet's chillingly unremorseful line after he has killed Polonius: 'I'll lug the guts into the neighbour room' (3.4.210), as well as Laertes' demand to see his father: 'I'll not be juggled with' (4.5.129). We might not take conscious note of it, but there are nonetheless a series of sounds that are associated with the death of Polonius – none of them respectful. Polonius does not 'squeak' or 'gibber', but 'hugger-mugger', 'lug', 'guts' and 'juggled' all evoke the discordant noise Shakespeare has led his audience to expect from curtailed funeral rites. This is the antithesis of the proper observances by which the dead should be remembered, as Laertes complains:

His means of death, his obscure funeral –
No trophy, sword nor hatchment o'er his bones,
No noble rite, nor formal ostentation –
Cry to be heard as 'twere from heaven to earth ...

(4.5.205–8)

A nobleman was entitled to a memorial that displayed his coat of arms, and the 'trophy, sword' and 'hatchment' were the appurtenances by which his status would be displayed. The absence of the rites of memory here itself makes a sound – a '[c]ry' for justice, and as Laertes interprets it, a call from on high to revenge.

Of course, the dead Polonius himself does not speak to Laertes to demand that he be remembered or avenged, perhaps because he does not need to since his son has, so to speak, already got the message. This is not so for Hamlet and, fortunately, unlike Horatio's gibbering Romans, his father's Ghost – while also responsible for some under-the-stage rumbling – is also capable of intelligible discourse:

HAMLET
        Thou coms't in such a questionable shape
        That I will speak to thee.

(1.4.43–4)

'[Q]uestionable' is, in this case, an archaism that means capable of responding to questions, although Shakespeare is also likely punning on our modern sense of the word to suggest that the Ghost is a rather dubious form of Hamlet's father. The metrical effect here of a tri-syllabic 'questionable' means that Hamlet must linger over this word in contrast with the rest of the words in that line.

Hamlet has vowed to risk death and madness by speaking to his father's ghost, but at the same time, he demands silence from the others who have seen it:

> If it assume my noble father's person
> I'll speak to it, though hell itself should gape
> And bid me hold my peace. I pray you all,
> If you have hitherto concealed this sight
> Let it be tenable in your silence still ...

(1.2.242–6)

Silence here becomes the crucible that holds the secret knowledge of the apparition; it is the structure that allows it to be made 'tenable'. This passage traverses various permutations of the speech/silence dichotomy: the compulsion to speak, the potential injunction to silence, and the silence of clandestine knowledge. Secrecy is a particular manifestation of silence – not simply the absence of speech, but rather the active, palpable presence of the unspoken.

Indeed, silences are not all the same. Death is an inert condition beyond speaking and thinking, which is quite different from being physically incapable of speech (as in, say, having had your tongue cut out) or, being like animals, devoid of human language altogether. Thus, Hamlet's phrase 'a beast that wants the discourse of reason' (1.2.150), would not apply to a mute person for whom the discourse of reason is available even without the physical capacity to express it. Rather, Hamlet speaks here of the cognitive powers of language that constitute rationality – thinking is, after all, essentially a matter of speaking to oneself. In so curtailing the rites of mourning for his father, his mother, Hamlet says, has shown less discursive capacity than an animal:

O God, a beast that wants discourse of reason
Would have mourned longer ...

(1.2.150–1)

Hamlet's final soliloquy returns to this theme. Human beings are different from animals because God has 'made us with such large discourse' (4.4.35).

There are moments in the play, too, when silence is indicative of internal, unspoken dialogue. This is especially important in relation to Hamlet who is Shakespeare's most thoughtful tragic hero. At Ophelia's grave, for example, Gertrude describes Hamlet's assault on Laertes as a brief outburst of insanity, which will soon subside into 'drooping' silence:

QUEEN

This is mere madness,
And thus awhile the fit will work on him.
Anon, as patient as the female dove
When that her golden couplets are disclosed,
His silence will sit drooping.

(5.1.273–7)

Earlier, the King used a similar image of Hamlet brooding like a bird on its eggs: '[H]is melancholy sits on brood' (3.1.164), but for Claudius, the 'hatch and the disclose' would 'be some danger' (3.1.165–6). In Gertrude's intensely lyrical image, however, it is not Hamlet who will literally sit and droop in the conventional attitude of melancholy, but rather his silence. Gertrude also contrasts his dejection with that of a dove. As editors who gloss these lines always inform us, doves lay two eggs, hence the twinned, golden, down-covered offspring. Arguably, however, 'golden couplets' connote not so much the details of ornithological reproduction as the song of the dove, or two beautiful (and perhaps sad) lines of lyric that, once sung, leave the singer downcast. In this interpretation, the passage becomes a brief meditation on the contrast and connection between poetry and silence.

Perhaps the silence that bears most fully upon the import of Hamlet's last line is the terrifying silence in the First Player's speech on the death of Priam, King of Troy. The narrative recounts the moment just before Pyrrhus kills the king. There is '*A silence in the heavens*' (2.2.422), the '*winds [are] speechless*' (2.2.423) and earth is '*As hush as death*' (2.2.424). This is not the ultimate silence of death – just the calm before the storm, the brutal murder of Priam. This episode from the ancient world is key because it serves, as we have seen earlier, as the play's template for revenge, and the silences in this passage work both to parallel and to counterpoint the silence at the end of the play. Is Hamlet's final silence, then, absolute, or is it like the pregnant pause before Pyrrhus renews his blows on Priam, merely an interlude before the action resumes with the arrival of Fortinbras? Hamlet's most politically potent pronouncement – his 'dying voice' (5.2.340) – has nominated Fortinbras as the next king of Denmark. Thus Hamlet's last words, which are not followed by any groaning or inarticulate death rattle (at least not in our Q2 text), seem to render his 'silence' as absolute.

Hamlet's last word speaks to the inadequacy of language to account for the violence and suffering of tragedy. The last word gestures to all that is beyond words. Directors and actors have to decide how to perform this scene, and readers must decide how to interpret it. Does Hamlet emit no dying groan at all? Does he just fall completely silent? There may have been some noise in Elizabethan performances – albeit presumably of a more sophisticated variety than that of the aforementioned squeaking and gibbering Romans – because the Folio text reads, 'The rest is silence. / O, O, O, O. Dies' (5.2.312–13). '*Dies*' is, of course, meant to be a stage direction, not something the actor actually says, but the repeated 'O' sounds are presumably Hamlet's last agonies. Whatever death may be – the transition to an 'undiscovered country from whose bourn / No traveller returns' (3.1.78–9)

– is not a silent business. It is, however, the point at which eloquence finally peters out.

Review

Above, we examined some key aspects of the play, as it were, from the writer's point of view, and we have looked under the hood to see how Shakespeare deployed specific poetic and rhetorical techniques to achieve certain dramatic effects. We have also been developing our own techniques as readers who want to write about the play. In particular, we have honed in on single words, tropes, figures of speech and specific passages as a way of understanding how Shakespeare uses poetic language to draw together the central themes of the play.

Writing matters

We focused in this chapter on two aspects of Shakespeare's language as a theme and as an idea, as well as on some of the more technical aspects of verse and rhetoric. Both of these are also useful ways for you to approach the play.

1   In the first section, I focused on one word: 'word'. (It was an obvious choice.) So now, over to you: pick a word, any word – well, almost any word. It's best if you choose a word that is in some way prominent in the text. Track your word through the course of the play and write about what you discover. What does concentrating on this particular word bring to your attention? Then, do some research on your word in the dictionary (the *OED* works best for this exercise and is online) and in a Shakespeare concordance (in which are listed all the uses of that particular word). A very useful online resource is David Crystal's Shakespeare

glossary http://www.shakespeareswords.com. Another
good idea is to use an online searchable Shakespeare
text, such as *Drama Online*, if your institution
subscribes to it: http://www.dramaonlinelibrary.com/

2   Sometimes when you find the language of the play
very difficult to understand, if you do a little digging,
you may discover that you are in good company.
Take the following: 'the dram of eale / Doth all the
noble substance of a doubt / To his own scandal –'
(1.4.36–8). The eighteenth-century Shakespeare editor
Theobald declared these lines to be so cryptic that he
deemed them indecipherable:

> In reality, I do not know a Passage, throughout all
> our Poet's Works, more intricate and deprav'd in
> the Text, of less Meaning to outward Appearance,
> or more likely to baffle the Attempts of Criticism
> in its Aid. It is certain, there is neither *Sense*,
> *Grammar*, nor *English*, as it now stands (qtd. in
> Thompson and Taylor, 205).

If you look at the passage in its context and avail
yourself of Thompson's and Taylor's editorial note,
you will discover that the general gist of it is that one
bad apple can contaminate another and bring it into
disrepute. Thus, you will need to look at more of the
scene (1.4.13–38). This very difficult expression, 'the
dram of eale', is part of a tough passage where Hamlet
opines about human nature. First, pick out what you
take to be the most obscure words and phrases – such
as 'viscious mole' and 'plausive manners' – and see
what you can make of them. Write your analysis of this
passage without trying to arrive at all possible definitive
meanings and interpretations. Instead, sit with the
uncertainties and complications and try to draw them
out. In other words, don't keep trying to pin down the

meaning, but experiment with opening it up, allowing for complexity and ambiguity without feeling pressed to resolve them into a cold, hard paraphrase.

3   I made the case throughout this chapter that the density and complexity of language is integral to *Hamlet*, not just some accretion on top of the plot that could be removed to make things easier. In light of this point, examine the following passage where Hamlet instructs Horatio to observe Claudius's reactions while watching the play. Then read the *No Fear Shakespeare* 'translation' below. Think about the idea of translation in this context as you compare and contrast the two, and write down your observations:

> There is a play tonight before the King –
> One scene of it comes near the circumstance
> Which I have told thee of my father's death.
> I prithee when thou seest that act afoot,
> Even with the very comment of thy soul
> Observe my uncle. If his occulted guilt
> Do not itself unkennel in one speech
> It is a damned ghost that we have seen
> And my imaginations are as foul
> As Vulcan's stithy. Give him heedful note,
> For I mine eyes will rivet to his face
> And after we will both our judgments join
> In censure of his seeming.

HORATIO   Well, my lord
> If 'a steal aught the whilst this play is playing
> And scape detected I will pay the theft.

> (3.2.71–85)

Sparknotes' No Fear Shakespeare modernizes this passage as follows:

> The point is, there's a play being performed for the

king tonight. One of the scenes comes very close to depicting the circumstances of my father's death, as I described them to you. Watch my uncle carefully when that scene begins. If his guilty secret does not reveal itself, then that ghost was just a devil, and my hunch wasn't, in fact, worth anything. Watch him closely. I'll stare at him too, and afterward we'll compare notes on him' and Horatio's reply as: 'My lord, I'll watch him as closely as I would a thief. I won't miss a trick.'

4 It's important to use detail when you write about big questions. It is also important sometimes to put small details of the text into a larger literary, historic or philosophical context. One of the questions I like to ask about all kinds of texts that deploy verse forms is, 'What is poetry for?' Consider, then, what the poetry is *for* in *Hamlet*. What does it do? What does it achieve? Clearly it isn't merely decorative (though that can be an important dimension of verse), but sometimes it is functional and instrumental. As you do this exercise, make sure you give concrete examples from the text.

CHAPTER THREE

Language through time

It is often said that *Hamlet* is timeless, but it is more accurate to say that the play belongs both to its own historical moment and to ours. *Hamlet* has not skimmed the surface of the years but, rather, has become enmeshed in the cultural fabric of every succeeding century since its composition. In 1600, *Hamlet* represented something completely new, perhaps most conspicuously in relation to Shakespeare's depiction of Hamlet's character. This chapter examines some of the major historical changes that were the context for Shakespeare's innovations in *Hamlet*.

The inquiries provoked by the play have also transformed over the years. The passage of time changes what readers and audiences see in the play since some issues move to the foreground of cultural consciousness while others recede from it. *Hamlet*'s remarkable powers are such that the play can draw on the energies of any given historical moment to renew its relevance. This process of regeneration is such that the *Hamlet* of tomorrow will be different from *Hamlet* today. Probably few readers would now concur with W. H. Auden's assessment that 'Ophelia is a silly, repressed girl and is obscene and embarrassing when she loses her mind over her father's death' (Auden, 162). Auden wrote prior to the advent of the women's movement of the 1970s and before feminist criticism, which looked afresh at Shakespeare's female characters as well as at the concept of gender more broadly.

Recently too, the war and political contestation that serve as motors for the play's action have become increasingly significant in both criticism and performance. The conflict with Norway, with which *Hamlet* opens, is no longer understood as merely the backdrop to the play's main events. Thus, developments surrounding political and military power and issues of gender have shaped contemporary ways of understanding *Hamlet*, and those developments will be the focus of the second part of this chapter.

1. Character: 'Naked' (4.7.49)

Contrary to the expectations of most modern readers, Claudius's line, "Tis Hamlet's character. "Naked"' (4.7.49) does not mean that Hamlet's character has been laid bare. Rather, in this line the King verifies that the letter announcing Hamlet's return to Denmark is indeed written in his nephew's handwriting, or his 'character'. The letter informs Claudius that Hamlet will arrive 'naked' – that is, not without clothes, but without armed support or military supplies. This quotation, however, also serves as an apt reminder that all literary characters are creatures of writing. While it should go without saying that characters are not real people, critics and readers have a tendency to discuss them as if they were not theatrical simulacra but rather as individuals with lives off-stage. This is the 'trick' of mimesis, of representation, which makes us mistake art for reality.

In the nineteenth century, Hamlet's character, the heart of his mystery, became the focus of critical attention. He was thought to be a poetic genius whose excruciating sensitivity made his life unbearable. He was almost the creature of a novel come to life rather than a character performed by an actor in a play. Indeed, this emphasis on Hamlet's character overshadowed every other aspect of the play to the extent that the play *Hamlet* and the character Hamlet became conflated with one another. In contrast, later twentieth-century critics have tended to stress the political, religious and social circumstances of the play in its entirety, even while acknowledging the power of its tragic protagonist.

Ways of understanding literary character, then, shift over time along with the representational conventions of a given literary period. Similarly, definitions of personhood are also subject to historical transformation. Both of these phenomena have had important implications for understanding Hamlet's character. For the nineteenth and much of the twentieth centuries, the predominant way of thinking about personhood was shaped by the ideas of *individualism*. Roughly speaking, individualism is the understanding of society as a collection of individuals with the attendant conviction that the individual, who is believed to possess an unfathomably deep and authentic inner being, takes precedence over the society as a whole. This is a vitally important idea in democratic cultures that seek to foster humanitarian values and safeguard personal freedoms. However, with the advent of postmodernist critiques of individualism, human beings began to be understood not as profound wells of interiority whose depths might be plumbed, but as 'subjects' who do not have an essential core. From a postmodern perspective, human identities are a product of the social, historical, political and even psychosexual discourses that have 'constructed' them. This may seem like an overly mechanical, even totalitarian, way of viewing human nature, but this is not invariably the case. At least in some understandings of postmodern subjectivity, *people* remain unfathomably complex and unique, but the emphasis falls on the intensely social character of the *subject* and on his or her necessary connectedness to political, institutional and ideological structures. To simplify, for good or ill, the 'individual' is thought to be self-sufficient while the 'subject' is thought to exist in connection with everyone else.

Despite these changing and divergent perspectives on character and selfhood among both readers and critics, there is a consensus that Shakespeare achieved something entirely new in *Hamlet*, and that the literary representation of characters – their thoughts, circumstances and sufferings – were taken to a completely new level through the play's tragic protagonist. Indeed, within the historical trajectory of both medieval mystery plays and the heavily didactic, allegorical drama of the morality tradition to the more complex characters of later literature, *Hamlet* constitutes a decisive turning point. *Hamlet*, as Stephen Greenblatt points out, 'seems to mark an epochal shift not only in Shakespeare's own career but in Western drama' (Greenblatt, *Norton*, 1685). Such a change would have been impossible through the vehicles of medieval mystery or miracle drama. These plays were religious in content and addressed the central moments in the vast timespan of biblical history from Creation to Doomsday. Such plays offered an account of history, as it were, from God's point of view. Medieval drama bequeathed to the Elizabethan stage characters that were largely one-dimensional. However, this was not only a result of the earlier period's different techniques of dramatic characterization, but it was also a consequence of medieval understandings of human identity itself. In the overwhelmingly static hierarchies of the medieval world, people were their social roles (their occupations), and roles were determined almost entirely by social status. Furthermore, there was very little sense of distance between a person's designated social function and the rest of their identity because social roles constituted the entirety of that identity. This above description of medieval personhood is no doubt an over-simplification, but since the goal here is to highlight how that had changed by the early modern period, it remains reasonably accurate to say that the medieval under-standing of personhood was essentially that of a role endowed with a soul. The soul was what remained when earthly life was over and would either fly up to heaven or fall down to hell. The tradition of the medieval morality play, such as the anonymous *Everyman* (c. 1520), dramatized exactly this inter-pretation of the human condition. Its residue is discernible, for example, in Hamlet's assertion that he will speak to the Ghost 'though hell itself should gape' (1.2.243). This is an allusion to the wide, gaping jaws of the mouth of hell, the conventional setting for the mystery plays. Literally a big mouth, complete with blazing torches that gave off smoke and sparks, this stage property was still in use in some early modern plays. When a sinner fell in hell's mouth, he would be swallowed up in the biblical manner: 'Therefore gapeth hell' (Isaiah 5.14, Bishop's Bible). This is the destination Claudius fears when he attempts – and fails – to implore divine mercy. His words 'fly up' (3.3.97) to heaven, but his 'limed' soul is like a bird caught in a snare that, 'struggling to be free / Art more engaged' (3.3.68–9). Claudius' internal battle is delineated as part of the cosmic battle between good and evil. His interiority thus unfolds like that of a medieval psychodrama where the good and evil angels battle it out for the Christian soul. Shakespeare is indebted to this tradition, but his characterizations also depart from it. The perversity of Claudius' sin and his failure to adequately repent make him a much more complex personality than the smooth hypocrite he otherwise seems. The big difference between Claudius and his medieval predecessors is that he has an interiority that they do not, and cannot, possess. For example, even when the devil of the medieval mystery plays was alone downstage bantering intimately and animatedly with the audience, there was no sense that he had an inner thought process or that there was anything baffling or indecipherable going on inside his mind because he really had no 'inside'– he was a flat character. In contrast, both Christian theology and fairly rigid stage conventions shaped the devil as a dramatic type in such a way that his motivations were dictated in advance, making his wickedness transparent and his actions entirely foreseeable. (God's motives were even more predictable because, unlike Satan, he was too holy even to surprise the audience with a good joke.) In contrast, despite being a Machiavellian schemer, Claudius has a conscience, and suffers an inner struggle with his conflicting impulses.

Once characters are endowed with complex interiority, one of the problems faced by the dramatist, as opposed to the novelist, is that there is no easy means to convey it. Unlike the playwright, the novelist has a handy first-person narrator at his or her disposal to express a character's thoughts and feelings. Therefore, to some degree the actor must embody them (through tone of voice, posture and so on), and what cues this embodiment is the playwright's language.

Hamlet's soliloquies, of course, provide more direct insight into his inner being, but Hamlet is a game changer in terms of dramatic representation – not only because the soliloquies offer insight into more of his interior being, but also because what is inside is radically different from his predecessors in the tradition of English drama. As Greenblatt has observed, '[I]t is as if the play were giving birth to a whole new kind of literary subjectivity. This subjectivity – the sense of being inside a character's psyche and following its twists and turns – is to a large degree an effect of language, the product of dramatic poetry and prose of unprecedented intensity' (Greenblatt, *Norton*, 1685). In *Hamlet*, Shakespeare approximates living, human identity in a way that even his more immediate theatrical predecessors did not. Marlowe's great tragic hero, Tamburlaine, for example, is much more of a role – a thundering, powerful presence – but he is not a character that the audience gets to know from the inside as we do Hamlet. Yet, Hamlet's soliloquies do not make him transparent to us. Indeed, critics have long noted that his 'To be or not to be' speech contains not a single personal pronoun, which makes these lines puzzling if we expect them to offer some autobiographical form of revelation. Soliloquies, however, do make Hamlet enigmatic in precisely the ways that real thoughts and motivations are often opaque and complicated. Hamlet has the *ineffable* within him – that is to say, he contains something which cannot be represented: 'I have that within which passes show' (1.2.85). It is precisely by suggesting what *cannot be represented* that Shakespeare inaugurates modern modes of characterization. *This* is what makes Hamlet seem more lifelike than anything else.

Philosophical Hamlet: 'What?' (1.5.110)

'Just do it!' is decidedly *not* Hamlet's motto. He refuses to be an action hero like Fortinbras because such characters are not thinkers but warriors who are focused on the glory of battle and not at all on the consequences and costs of violence. In contrast, Hamlet's capacity to consciously reflect upon the nature of his own consciousness is one of the most compelling qualities of his characterization. In this way, *Hamlet* predates and yet uncannily anticipates the seventeenth-century philosopher René Descartes' famous dictum, '*Cogito ergo sum*,' 'I think therefore I am' (Descartes, 61). Descartes argued that the very capacity for thought both defined and constituted human consciousness. One might go so far as to say that the centuries of philosophy since Descartes have revolved around the capacity of human consciousness to engage in self-examination, that is, to take itself as its own object. A key dimension of this aspect of philosophy, and one particularly pertinent to *Hamlet*, is that the capacity for self-reflexive consciousness does not in and of itself have any impact – let alone any beneficial influence – on the world around it. That is, the lucidity of human consciousness is not only somewhat disconnected from the outside world, but it also cannot alter the human predicament of which it is so excruciatingly self-aware: that its destination is mortality. Indeed, it is arguably this – the knowledge of our own mortality – that is the defining feature of self-reflexive consciousness.

Hamlet's character is distinguished by precisely this philosophical disposition. In his soliloquies, he asks the same questions that philosophers have pondered for millennia: what is the nature of human consciousness? What do we know of the world? That last question, in fact, constitutes an entire branch of philosophy known as 'epistemology', the theory of knowledge. What is our connection to the divine, to the cosmos, and to all that we do not and cannot know? As he tells Horatio: 'There are more things in heaven and earth, Horatio, / Than are dreamt of in your philosophy' (1.5.165–6). Questions about what we know of the world take very specific forms in *Hamlet*: how can Hamlet know whether the Ghost is from heaven or hell and whether it speaks the truth? How can he prove that Claudius is guilty? How can he know whether his mother committed adultery or if she conspired in his father's murder? Only when he is 'antic' – that is, genuinely or feignedly out of his wits – does Hamlet's dominant mode of speaking become the statement rather than the question. In such instances, it is more often the case that other characters question *him*. Consider, for example, when Hamlet is in his mother's closet, and he sees the Ghost who remains invisible to her: 'To whom do you speak this?' (3.4.27), or when he befuddles Claudius who asks confusedly, 'What dost thou mean by this?' (4.3.28).

Montaigne's scepticism

In the history of philosophy, it is generally assumed that an animal, or 'a beast that wants discourse of reason' (1.2.150), does not ponder the nature of its own existence and is therefore ignorant of its inevitable death. There have been a few exceptions to this general run of human arrogance, such as the great French thinker and essayist, Michel de Montaigne (1533–92), author of *The Essays or Moral, Politic and Military Discourses of Lord Michel de Montaigne*, which was translated into English by John Florio in 1603. Montaigne is especially associated with scepticism – a philosophical mode of inquiry that proceeds by doubting and questioning all received wisdom. He famously inquired: 'When I am playing with my cat, who knows whether she have more sport in dallying with me than I have in gaming with her?' (Greenblatt, ed., *Shakespeare's Montaigne: The Florio Translation*, 142). Although Florio's translation was printed in 1603, it was licensed for publication in 1601, which suggests that Florio would have been working on it around the same time that Shakespeare was composing *Hamlet*. What is more interesting is that there is very likely a personal connection between Shakespeare and Florio, since Florio was the tutor to Shakespeare's patron, the Earl of Southampton. In writing *The Tempest*, Shakespeare took a passage directly from Montaigne's *Essays*, but while that kind of evidence does not exist for his influence on *Hamlet*, we do know that the influence of Montaigne's thought, though not yet translated from the French, had already reached London, and that his ideas and writings were in circulation there. Scholars disagree about the degree of influence that Montaigne had on *Hamlet*. George Coffin Taylor's *Shakespeare's Debt to Montaigne* (1925) argued for specific verbal parallels between the *Essays* and Shakespeare's play. There is a much more plausible case to be made for the philosophical similarities between *Hamlet* and Montaigne than there is for specific verbal coincidence. Hamlet's self-awareness, as well as his curiosity about and questioning of the human condition, is very much of a piece with Montaigne. What is crucial here is that Montaigne offered a new way of thinking about the world and the self that was a decided departure from medieval thought. Prior to the Protestant Reformation, all of Europe shared a single religious conviction – that of the Roman Catholic Church – and this orthodoxy tended towards a monolithic worldview that was shattered by the combined forces of the intellectual and technological developments synonymous with both the Renaissance and the religious ruptures of the Reformation. As a result of scientific developments and voyages into hitherto unknown parts of the world, horizons were expanded – both literally and metaphorically – when Copernicus and Galileo overturned Ptolemaic assumptions that the earth was flat and was the centre of the universe. Alarmingly, this might also have meant that Earth and all the people living on it were not, in fact, the apples of God's eye. This new way of thinking encouraged the questioning of even the most fundamental assumptions: the very ground on which people stood (was it flat or round?) became uncertain and thus a matter for debate. In *Hamlet*, this new spirit of determined inquiry is reflected in its very opening question, 'Who's there?' (1.1.1), as well as in Hamlet's subsequent pensive and intellectually probing expressions of scepticism. Because early modern systems of punctuation were not at all regularized, some famous questions in *Hamlet*, such as, 'To be or not to be' (3.1.55) and 'What piece of work is a man' (2.2.269), are not followed by question marks. Hamlet's interrogative mode ranges from his inquiry into the human impulse to seek social status despite impending mortality, '[W]hy of that loam whereto he [Alexander] was converted / might they not stop a beer-barrel?' (5.1.200–1) to matter-of-fact questions, such as, 'Who is this they follow? / And with such maimed rites? (5.1.207–8), and '[W]ilt thou know / Th'effect of what I wrote?' (5.2.36–7).

Other characters in the play operate within different, non-interrogative registers. For example, Polonius does not think much beyond the most pragmatic horizons. When he is in philosophical mode, Polonius rehearses established ethical precepts, urging Laertes 'to thine own self be true' (1.3.77). Similarly, Rosencrantz rather sycophantically recapitulates Renaissance political theory on the nature and significance of sovereignty for Claudius' benefit. Because it is synonymous with the body politic and the whole realm, the king's life, Rosencrantz argues, must be preserved at all costs: 'That spirit upon whose weal depends and rests / The lives of many' (3.3.14–15). Notably, the women in *Hamlet* do not discourse on philosophy or political theory. Their privileged mode of utterance, as we shall see, is lyric, which, far from being inferior, constitutes some of the most beautiful language in *Hamlet*.

The deeply reflective quality that is embodied by Hamlet's character finds its analogue in the capacity of theatre to reflect upon its own representational strategies. Hamlet illustrates this very often throughout the play – sometimes by figuring himself as an actor: '[T]hey are actions that a man might play' (1.2.84). Nowhere does Shakespeare demonstrate more clearly that art, specifically drama, facilitates and objectifies the capacity of human consciousness to reflect upon itself than in the play-within-the-play, the vehicle through which Claudius' perfidy is revealed. Despite the vexed relationship between thought and action, Hamlet is in no doubt about the political and emotional impact of theatre, which can discover the King's guilt and lay bare all that has been concealed.

Describing Hamlet: (2.1.74–97)

For all of Hamlet's interiority, he is also described by other characters, for example, as 'a noble mind' (3.1.149) and 'The glass of fashion' (3.1.152). One of the most remarkable perspectives on Hamlet from the outside in occurs in Ophelia's account of how Hamlet, distraught and deranged, visited her while she was sewing in her 'closet' (2.1.74) or private chamber:

> Lord Hamlet, with his doublet all unbraced,
> No hat upon his head, his stockings fouled,
> Ungartered and down-gyved to his ankle,
> Pale as his shirt, his knees knocking each other,
> And with a look so piteous in purport
> As if he had been loosed out of hell
> To speak of horrors, he comes before me.

(2.1.75–81)

Marjorie Garber has called this episode an 'unscene', or 'unseen', because it is described rather than performed (Garber, 35). What does Shakespeare achieve by this? Garber argues that this episode is represented 'at one remove, leaving the actual words and gestures of the participants to the audience's imagination, while vividly underscoring the emotional significance of what has taken place' (Garber, 43). In Act 1, Hamlet warns Horatio that, 'hereafter', he may seem 'strange or odd' (1.5.168) if he thinks it 'meet / To put an antic disposition on' (1.5.169–70). If he is only pretending to be melancholic or mad during his exchange with Ophelia, however, then he has been alarmingly convincing. He has just seen the Ghost when he visits her, and being pale as his shirt is not something he could achieve by pretence – unless, that is, he is a very good actor. That is always possible, especially if we consider the Player's performance of Hecuba: '– Tears in his eyes, distraction in his aspect' (2.2.490). However, because the 'unscene' occurs in a 'closet', and because it is a reported incident, rather than one the audience actually sees, one does not get the impression that Hamlet is 'faking it'. Certainly, whether or not Hamlet was acting, Ophelia clearly experienced Hamlet's visit as a genuine revelation of the extent of his sufferings, and perhaps even an abortive attempt to share them with her. Save for a shattering 'sigh so piteous and profound' (2.1.91), this is, according to Ophelia, a silent encounter. Hamlet is literally undone. He is hatless, or 'unbraced', and 'down-gyved', – that is, his dirty stockings are down around his ankles – and he exhibits all the sartorial symptoms of extreme distress.

Ophelia's speech functions as a kind of hearsay. The audience has not witnessed Hamlet in this condition directly for themselves. Although Hamlet was in a state of apparent terror, he nonetheless used force on Ophelia: 'He took me by the wrist and held me hard' (2.1.84), and he constrained her for (so to speak) the space of ten lines: 'That done, he lets me go' (2.1.93). We have no reason to doubt Ophelia, but the play now requires the audience to put this description together with those aspects of Hamlet that they have experienced directly. Far from pinning down Hamlet's character, the 'unscene', which functions almost like a dumb show, opens it up or dilates it, to reveal that his relationship with Ophelia is marked both by violence and deep ambiguity.

2. Power and gender

Power: 'This warlike state' (1.2.8–9)

Hamlet is a tragedy not just because its tragic hero is killed and it ends with bodies piled up around him, but also because Hamlet does not inherit the Danish throne, which is instead ceded to the bellicose prince of Norway, Fortinbras. As 'Th'expectation and rose of the fair state' (3.1.151), Hamlet, as Fortinbras acknowledges at the play's end, 'was likely, had he been put on, / To have proved most royal' (5.2.381–2). This is important because one of the key dimensions of the genre of tragedy, both classical and Elizabethan, is that its concern with suffering was confined to those of high estate, to the aristocratic class who in this era had a monopoly over political power. The idea of a ghost appearing to some lowly person to demand revenge would have seemed ludicrous to an early modern audience since, from the point of view of a rigidly hierarchized society, there would be nothing at stake – no crown, no 'imperial jointress' (1.2.9) – for the lowly person to avenge. Around the time Shakespeare was writing *Hamlet*, a new subgenre known as domestic tragedy was beginning to develop. Plays within this genre, such as the anonymous *Arden of Faversham*, *A Warning for Fair Women*, *A Yorkshire Tragedy* (attributed to Thomas Middleton) and Thomas Heywood's *A Woman Killed With Kindness* involved protagonists who were neither the nation's elite nor its impoverished but, rather, merchants and small landowners. The genre appropriate to the lowest echelons of society remained comedy because the sufferings of those who did not own property simply did not conform to any received concept of tragedy. Tragedy still belonged primarily to political elites because the genre was fundamentally, as J.W. Lever puts it in the title of his book, *The Tragedy of State*.

   Shakespeare does, of course, represent family dynamics in *Hamlet*, but these constitute the inner workings of what is fundamentally a dynastic rather than domestic tragedy because the fate of Hamlet and his family is also the fate of the nation. Laertes cautions his sister:

> His greatness weighed, his will is not his own.
> He may not, as unvalued persons do,
> Carve for himself, for on his choice depends
> The safety and health of this whole state ...

> (1.3.17–20)

Although no one in the royal household seems to consider Ophelia an inappropriate match for the heir to the throne, Laertes insists that Hamlet's marriage must be a dynastic alliance rather than one of personal choice. Even more importantly, the death of the sovereign changes the destiny of the state: 'The cess [cease] of majesty / Dies not alone, but like a gulf doth draw / What's near it with it" (3.3.15–17).

High politics

While most of the plot is concerned with very specific, personal incidences of murderous conflict, its larger context is the recent war between Denmark and Norway and the enmity with Poland. The Ghost appears in warlike aspect wearing the armour he wore during the battle with the Norwegian king, and '[s]o frowned he once, when in an angry parle / He smote the sledded Polacks on the ice' (1.1.61–2). The single-syllabled verb 'smote' conveys the sense of the axe coming down on the multi-syllabled 'sledded Polacks', reaching a deadly termination in 'ice'. While such belligerence may be appropriate to battle, it might not be to 'parle', usually a negotiation towards an end to the fighting. (Since negotiators typically do not kill one another, the dead king and his kin-slaying brother may have more in common than we might expect). In Act 1, Denmark's 'implements of war' (1.1.73) are being readied for its renewed hostilities toward Norway since Fortinbras now seeks to recover the lands his father forfeited to the Danes. However, we learn in Act 2 that in Norway, the brother of the dead king (Fortinbras of Norway) has also succeeded to the throne rather than his son, Young Fortinbras, the current king's nephew. The Norwegian king has discovered that his nephew planned to attack Denmark and that the king has intervened to prevent it. Instead, young Fortinbras requests safe passage through Denmark in order to attack Poland. This is a worthless conflict, as the Norwegian Captain admits: 'We go to gain a little patch of ground / That hath in it no profit but the name' (4.4.17–18). That these are the political decisions made by the man who will, at the end of the play, become the new ruler of Denmark makes its resolution an uneasy one. On the other hand, concord between Denmark and England is also an important part of the plot and allows Claudius to send Hamlet to England with Rosencrantz and Guildenstern. However, Claudius relies on the English King to do his bidding only because England has apparently recently felt the might of 'the Danish sword' (4.3.59).

There is in *Hamlet* conflict both between nations and within the Danish state itself. As Marcellus so famously puts it, 'Something is rotten in the state of Denmark' (1.4.90). The play's repetition of disease imagery suggests a kind of fetid putrefaction that allows Horatio's line 'some strange eruption in our state' (1.1.168) to imply political turbulence as well as a septic boil. This 'eruption' afflicts not only the body politic, which refers to government in general, but also the physical body of the king, with which it is synonymous. When, as the Ghost reports, Claudius poured the 'leperous distilment' (1.5.64) into his brother's ear, he simultaneously administered poison to the body politic that now festers with corruption:

And a most instant tetter barked about
Most lazar-like with vile and loathsome crust
All my smooth body.

Thus was I sleeping by a brother's hand
Of life, of crown, of queen at once dispatched ...

(1.5.71–5)

King Hamlet's body thus became afflicted with something like an instantly fatal leprosy. He didn't just die; he died with a truly hideous skin condition, with an outbreak of 'tetter' that the Ghost elaborates on as a 'loathsome crust' of bark-like scabs (note that the alliterative 'l's in 'lazar-like' and 'loathsome' almost allow us to see the corruption spreading).

Despite having ascended the throne by regicide, from an early modern point of view, once Claudius becomes king, removing him from it would be both illegal and morally wrong. Even though it did not save his brother, Claudius is banking on the doctrine of the Divine Right of Kings to protect him. This is the theory that no matter what crooked path the sovereign took to reach the throne, and no matter how many dead bodies he stepped on to get there, once crowned, the king's sovereignty was upheld by God himself: 'There's such divinity doth hedge a king / That treason can but peep' (4.5.123–4). This system meant that those in power were perpetually insecure – and indeed, in early modern Europe, assassination was not an uncommon route to power. A further consequence of this structural problem in relation to succession was that the insecurity of those in power bred surveillance and espionage, or 'seeing unseen' (3.1.32). Polonius sets Reynaldo to spy on Laertes in Paris; Claudius sets Rosencrantz and Guildenstern on Hamlet, and Claudius himself scrutinizes Hamlet: '[We] shall sift him' (2.2.58).

The play, however, leaves us with additional questions about power in Denmark. For example, would Claudius still have been a usurper, or would he have been the legitimate ruler of Denmark had his brother died of natural causes? What kind of monarchy is Denmark? Is it like England where a model of primogeniture prevailed – that is, where the eldest male inherits? Hamlet certainly complains that his uncle has

'[p]opped in between th'election and my hopes' (5.2.63).
Or is Denmark, like some European monarchies, an elective
monarchy? (Note, however, that election was nothing like
our modern system of voting in a democracy.) Certainly, this
appears to be the case in neighbouring Norway where young
Fortinbras' uncle has inherited the throne. The play does
not resolve the issues surrounding the right to monarchical
succession. Claudius has named Hamlet, who is 'the most
immediate to our throne' (1.2.109) as his heir, but Hamlet,
who knows that his uncle has committed regicide, still looks
to his deceased father as the ultimate and only legitimate
authority. He uses his paternal inheritance to the throne
decisively when he rewrites the warrant commanding his
execution while aboard the ship bound for England:

I had my father's signet in my purse –
Which was the model of that Danish seal –

(5.2.49–50)

This is one of the most important political acts in the play
because it is by claiming his father's authority that Hamlet,
at last, begins to achieve autonomy and escapes the snare
Claudius has set for him.

Hamlet the assassin

One uncanny historical intersection between the play's
rehearsal of murder as a form of political intervention and
actual political events is that it was an actor who had played
Hamlet, John Wilkes Booth, who assassinated President
Abraham Lincoln.

While his theatrical successes were subsequently obscured
by his nefarious role in American history, John Wilkes
Booth had distinguished himself as a talented actor whose
roles included Hamlet and Julius Caesar. His brother, one
of the most famous Hamlets of all time, Edwin Booth, was

a supporter of Lincoln, and while on April 14, 1865 John Wilkes was shooting Lincoln at Ford's Theatre in Washington DC, Edwin was in Boston enacting Hamlet's hesitation about murdering the ruler of the realm. Lincoln's assassination was a tragic and notorious episode at the end of the American Civil War, but from the point of view of understanding and inter-preting *Hamlet*, it is more than just an interesting historical tid-bit. Rather, this momentous event speaks to one of the central problems of the play, namely whether or not it is ever right to depose – or even kill – the ruler of the realm.

In November of 1864, the same month that *Hamlet* had opened at the Winter Garden Theatre in New York City with Edwin Booth in the title role, there had been a heated election in which the Democratic candidate General George McClellan challenged Lincoln. McClellan sought peace with the South, even if it meant continuing slavery. It is little wonder that this production of *Hamlet* ran for a record-setting one hundred performances. The play's themes were especially resonant since the city was one of the most 'copperhead' places in the North – that is, sympathetic to Southerners and desirous of a compromise to end the war.

Although the political situation of nineteenth-century America was worlds away from that of early modern England, there was still considerable common ground between them. All early modern monarchs feared assassination, but Elizabeth had even more reason to fear after her excommunication by the Pope who deemed her a heretic in 1570. Essentially, the Pope gave Catholics permission to depose her. Thus, in pre-democratic societies the question about whether a corrupt ruler could be justifiably killed was an urgent one. Apart from the charge of incest, Claudius is guilty beyond doubt of all he has been accused of: 'a vice of kings, / A cutpurse of the empire and the rule' (3.4.96–7) and '– a king of shreds and patches –' (3.4.99). Even as his wife falls, dying from the poisoned cup, he still tries to cover himself by saying that it is just a fainting fit: 'She swoons to see them bleed' (5.2.293). Up until the point where the dying Gertrude says she had been poisoned, Hamlet has hesitated about regicide, the gravest of crimes. The lords remind the audience of the indelibly political issues involved in killing Claudius when they shout, 'Treason, treason!' (5.2.307). This occurs just at the moment when Laertes reveals that 'the King, the King's to blame' (5.2.305) and as Hamlet stabs Claudius. As modern readers and audiences, we may forget this important political dimension of the play, but it would have been foremost in the minds of Shakespeare's contemporaries. While in the standard revenge narrative, murdering a reigning monarch may be par for the course, in a politically charged revenge play like *Hamlet*, hesitation before deciding to kill a king is strongly advised. Less than 50 years after *Hamlet* was written, the English did kill their anointed monarch. On 30 January 1649, King Charles I was beheaded at Whitehall.

Hierarchy: 'Here's fine revolution' (5.1.85)

In Act 5, events at last fully unfold to reach their desolate termination in the death of the Prince. Despite working within the generic confines of tragedy, Shakespeare begins Act 5 – the prelude to the tragic denouement – with the comedic exchange of the Gravediggers. They provide some relief from the impending tragic culmination of the play as well as a profound meditation on the nature of death itself. The Gravediggers' scene is also, however, a commentary on class hierarchy, the most fundamental of political structures in Shakespeare's day. Delving in the earth was quite literally one of the lowest forms of manual labour as Hamlet implicity acknowledges when he refers to the Gravedigger as 'this ass' (5.1.74). Yet, it is from this location that Shakespeare chooses to suggest the undoing of class hierarchy.

Because she seems to have committed suicide, from the perspective of early modern religious orthodoxy, Ophelia is guilty of a mortal sin worthy of eternal damnation. Despite this, the coroner has ruled that she can be buried in hallowed ground. '[T]his law' (5.1.21), or ruling, is, as the second gravedigger recognizes, purely a consequence of class privilege. This is the occluded 'truth 'on't' (5.1.23): 'If this had not been a gentlewoman she should have been buried out o'Christian burial' (5.1.23–5). This discussion is followed by an issue that must have been very close to Shakespeare's heart because it concerns the business of getting a coat of arms, which divided 'great folk' (5.1.27) from the commoners who made up the vast majority of the population:

> GRAVEDIGGER   There is no ancient
>   gentlemen but gardeners, ditchers and grave-makers.
>   They hold up Adam's profession.
> 2 MAN   Was he a gentleman?
> GRAVEDIGGER   'A was the first that ever bore arms.
>
> (5.1.29–33).

Shakespeare had finally succeeded in becoming wealthy enough to be granted arms on behalf of his father in 1596. Because this status was hereditary, Shakespeare himself also became a gentleman, though of course he was not born one. As Shakespeare knew, achieving the status of a gentleman was an immensely expensive, complicated and drawn-out process. Application to the College of Arms entailed, among many other steps, investigation and adjudication by the heralds of the College before an armorial design, the coat of arms, was assigned. (Shakespeare's design is a visual pun – a spear.) As a result the one-on-one combat between their kings, Norway's forfeiture of land to Denmark was '[w]ell ratified by law and heraldry' (1.1.86). As we saw in the previous chapter, Pyrrhus, the terrifying epitome of heroic revenge, is described in Act 2 in the language of heraldry. Whereas in Virgil his armour is dazzling, in Hamlet it is black or, to use the vocabulary of armorial design, 'sable'. Symbolically, then, the human cost of Pyrrhus' arms is incalculable.

However, the entire system of heraldry and hierarchy is turned on its head in the Gravediggers' scene. The Gravedigger's joke is that, as the first human being, Adam had arms in the physical sense of limbs, but the more incisive suggestion here is that the status conferred by grants of arms is neither God-given nor natural. This is significant because the predominant ideological spin on status was that it was naturally and divinely decreed. Such rationalizations are exposed here as entirely manufactured by a powerful elite. This is 'the truth' that the second gravedigger demands, albeit through the indirect language of comedy. Furthermore, this truth is almost fully obscured by social practices. A proverbial rhyme from the era rehearses the same political terrain as the Gravediggers' conversation:

> When Adam delved and Eve span,
> Who was then the gentleman?

> (Thompson and Taylor, 412).

Some 40 years after Shakespeare wrote *Hamlet*, during the British Civil Wars, sects like the Diggers, whose name also referred to people who worked the earth with spades, also drew on similar ideas of essential, primordial class equality.

The Gravedigger's reference to Adam is later echoed by Hamlet. He observes that the Gravedigger shows no reverence for mortal remains, hurling a skull about 'as if 'twere / Cain's jawbone, that did the first murder' (5.1.72–3). This 'first corpse' (1.2.105) was Abel, the son of Adam and Eve. Like Hamlet's father, Abel was murdered by his brother, Cain. The weapon in this case was the jawbone of an ass. Fratricide, or as Claudius puts it, 'A brother's murder' (3.3.38), is thus the first tragedy in Judeo-Christian history. Only one generation out of the utopian harmony of the Garden of Eden, 'the truth on't' revealed by this biblical episode is arguably that this ugly, murderous jockeying for power is an innate and indelible component of human nature.

Hamlet continues the social critique begun by the grave-diggers by pursuing a philosophical inquiry into the ephemeral nature of social status in contrast to the great levelling reality of death. Here, Hamlet's rhyme speaks of the futility of worldly power:

> Imperious Caesar, dead and turned to clay,
> Might stop a hole to keep the wind away.

> (5.1.202–3)

Throughout the play, references to Julius Caesar and Rome function as analogues to events in Elsinore. Political assassination in Rome was a result of Brutus' conspiracy, as it might have been (though we do not know one way or the other) of Gertrude's with Claudius. Caesar was not murdered as a result of an uprising of the masses but of the conspiracy of the political elite. There are in the play intimations of a significant upper echelon of government – 'the main voice of Denmark' (1.3.27) as well as references to the commoners, who constitute a potential menace to established authority largely because they outnumber those who govern. For example, Claudius worries about Hamlet's popularity: 'the great love the general gender [common people] bear him' (4.7.19). Shifts in power make 'the people muddied' (4.5.81) – that is, the populace becomes uncertain as to who is in charge. When Laertes returns to Elsinore, the people acknowledge him as their leader: 'Choose we: Laertes shall be king!' (4.5.106). The cry 'Choose we' is important because in early modern societies, 'the people' did not select their monarchs. When the populace threaten authority they become 'rabble': 'The rabble call him [Laertes] lord' (4.5.102). The fear of being potentially overwhelmed by sheer numbers leads to Claudius's concern that Laertes' 'rebellion looks so giant-like' (4.5.121).

As Hamlet says in the graveyard, 'Here's fine revolution an we had the / trick to see't' (5.1.85–6). 'Revolution' meant the complete inversion of the existing social order, and what was known as 'the world turned upside down', or 'topsy-turvey', was the early modern figure for the reversal of class hierarchy – the bottom were placed on the top, and vice versa. Carnivals and comedy were the licensed vehicles for this temporary inversion of social order, whose ultimate containment was a given – at least until the English Revolution. Why does Hamlet say we need a trick, a knack, to see it? Perhaps a 'trick' was required because power hierarchies were habitually understood to be completely natural. Viewed from below, however, from the grave and the netherworld of death, they are merely elaborate artifices, which only distract human beings from the ultimate destination of human life. The 'trick' of which Hamlet speaks also has an analogue in anamorphic or 'trick' painting, one of the new ways of playing with perspective that was developed in the Renaissance. A profile portrait of Edward VI (c. 1546), completed the year before he ascended the throne, probably by William Scrots, requires the viewer to position him or herself very precisely in order to see it properly. The most famous example of anamorphic painting, however, is that of the skull in the foreground of Hans Holbein's *The Ambassadors* (1533). Here death looms large for those who have the trick to see it – otherwise, it looks like an odd object floating in front of the painting's subjects.

The play, then, presents us with the 'trick' to see 'revolution', that is, the threat posed by the mass of people to those who govern and perhaps oppress them. The Gravediggers' scene serves as a reminder of the forced labour of the men in Act 1 who are given no respite even for religious observances, 'whose sore task / Does not divide the Sunday from the week' (1.1.74–5), and of the destitute Norwegians who enlist in Fortinbras' army merely to secure 'food and diet' (1.1.98).

Whores and harlots

Although much impressed by Hamlet's language, D. H. Lawrence was not at all impressed by Hamlet's character as he records in the poem, 'When I read Shakespeare':

> And Hamlet, how boring, how boring to live with,
> so mean and self-conscious, blowing and snoring
> his wonderful speeches, full of other folk's whoring!

The whore, the woman who is for sale, is a preoccupation of *Hamlet*, and not only that of the Prince himself. For example, when Claudius ponders his concealed sin, he considers himself as a prostitute:

> The harlot's cheek beautied with plastering art
> Is not more ugly [in relation] to the thing that helps
>   [covers] it
> Than is my deed to my most painted word.

$$(3.1.50–2)$$

We have already addressed some of the implications of Claudius's 'painted word' in terms of the opposition between words and deeds, but when we examine this metaphor in the context of the early modern condemnation of women's 'painting' (cosmetics) as a form of deception designed to ensnare men, as well as to hide venereal disease, the lines become powerful evidence of his deception. Hamlet has also accused Ophelia of being a painted lady, that is to say a (literally) two-faced whore: 'I have heard of your paintings well enough. / God hath given you one face and you make yourselves / another' (3.1.141–3). As Farah Karim-Cooper points out, 'Hamlet is constantly associating painting and tinctures with female, sexual and political corruption' (Karim-Cooper, 222). Hamlet makes another point related to this in the graveyard scene: 'Now get you to my lady's / table and tell her, let her paint an inch thick, to this / favour she must come. Make her laugh at that' (5.1.182–4). The misogynistic premise here is that women deliberately conceal a rancid, festering interior, and since Hamlet has recently bullied his mother into looking at a real or metaphoric mirror – 'a glass / Where you may see the inmost part of you' (3.4.18–19) – this jibe may be directed once again at Gertrude rather than at some merely generic courtly lady.

Certainly, Hamlet accuses his mother of trying to hide moral decay when, like a tub-thumping moralist he urges her, 'for love of grace' (3.4.142), to confess and repent the 'sin' of marrying Claudius. Unlike the way harlots apply cosmetics so that the substance is opaque and plastered on, in this instance, there is only a thin film of skin, which barely covers the pus and decay:

> Lay not that flattering unction to your soul
> That not your trespass but my madness speaks.
> It will but skin and film the ulcerous place
> Whiles rank corruption mining all within
> Infects unseen.

(3.4.143–7)

Although Gertrude may topically apply 'flattering unction' to her skin, this can be only a superficial remedy. Something gruesome is still 'mining', or burrowing, away beneath the epidermis. The harlot and Gertrude are indeed sisters under the skin. According to Hamlet, the moment Claudius took Gertrude between those 'incestuous sheets', he made her a whore: 'He that hath killed my King and whored my mother' (5.2.63). Nor is it clear which of these is the worse crime from Hamlet's point of view, even though the Ghost has told him not to pursue recriminations against the Queen:

> But howsomever thou pursues this act
> **Taint** not thy mind nor let thy soul contrive
> Against thy mother aught; leave her to heaven …

(1.5.84–6)

This is a little like the saying, 'Whatever you do, don't think about elephants.' Hamlet's thoughts become similarly absorbed by his mother's sexual transgression, although they were already tending toward that direction even before the Ghost's appearance. All the play's avengers have lost their fathers, but only Hamlet has lost his mother to what he perceives to be whoredom: 'How stand I then / That have a father killed, a mother **stained**' (4.4.55–6). The imagistic connection between Hamlet's 'taint' and Gertrude's 'stain' marks another level of connection between mother and son. The taint of adultery follows Gertrude, even though the play does not tell us for certain whether or not she was guilty of it. In contrast, Laertes' mother (who seems to be deceased) remained true to her marriage vows:

> That drop of blood that's calm proclaims me bastard,
> Cries 'Cuckold!' to my father, brands the harlot
> Even here between the chaste unsmirched brow
> Of my true mother.

(4.5.116–19)

Laertes worries for his 'true mother's' reputation. He argues that her virtue will be impugned if any portion of his being is not consumed with ire because that would constitute evidence of his illegitimacy. Laertes' reasoning is as follows: dutiful sons avenge their fathers' deaths while undutiful ones do not, *and* in that event, their mothers must be to blame. Revenge is thus a matter of proving legitimacy. Laertes' revenge, in contrast to that of Hamlet, derives from a concern to exonerate his mother from the stigma of adultery and his father from the ignominy of being a cuckold (a man betrayed by his wife). The cuckold is a figure who wears horns on his forehead that only he fails to see, while the brand in the middle of the woman's forehead is a reference to the practice of branding prostitutes. The latter punishment was never, in fact, practised in England though legislation to implement it was proposed in Parliament.

This is the only time Laertes' and Ophelia's mother is mentioned in the play, and only to affirm her son's legitimacy and thus his father's honour. However, the reference to her offers a powerful delineation of the gender dynamics of revenge.

Widows

Twenty-first century audiences may not attach much significance to Gertrude's status as a recent widow. In early modern England, however, a much greater percentage of the population suffered the death of a spouse prior to old age than today, and many women were widowed as often as twice or more in a lifetime. As a result, the issue of whether or not widows should remarry became one of the hot topics in the period's on-going debate about the status of women, known as the *querelle des femmes*. Some of the opprobrium attached to women who remarried arose from patriarchal concern about the financial autonomy they possessed as heirs to their husbands' wealth and property. Economic independence gave women the means, which they would not have had when they married for the first time, to choose a new spouse to their own liking, as opposed to marrying someone approved (and at times, actually chosen) by their families. A woman's second marriage was thus very different from her first. In the latter, her father controlled whatever dowry (consisting of money, land or other property) she might have brought to her first husband. While remarriage among early modern widows was not unusual, such women were subject to caricature and condemnation. So-called 'lusty widows' were believed to regard the demise of a husband as simply a positive opportunity to satisfy their own excessive carnal cravings. As a remarried widow, then, Gertrude conforms to a cultural stereotype.

The Ghost's complaint against Gertrude is ambiguous. It is unclear whether the Ghost is accusing her of adultery or merely complaining that she did not remain a perpetual widow. The implication of the Ghost's speech is that his fidelity, 'the vow / I made to her in marriage' (1.5.49–50), was not matched by his wife's during their marriage, and that while Gertrude shared his 'celestial bed' (1.5.56), she was simultaneously seeking sexual satisfaction elsewhere:

> O Hamlet, what falling off was there,
> From me whose love was of that dignity
> That it went hand in hand even with the vow
> I made to her in marriage, and to decline
> Upon a wretch whose natural gifts were poor
> To those of mine.
> But Virtue, as it never will be moved
> Though Lewdness court it in a shape of heaven,
> So Lust, though to a radiant angel linked,
> Will sate itself in a celestial bed
> And prey on garbage.

> (1.5.47–58)

As daughters of Eve, as they were known, all women were seen to bear the blame for the Fall from paradise because Eve listened to the serpent in the Garden of Eden and encouraged Adam to eat the forbidden fruit of the tree of knowledge. For hundreds of years, women bore the brunt of the stain of original sin that had resulted from that first transgression. Women were, from the period's theological point of view, responsible for the Fall from grace and innocence – the original 'falling off' (1.5.47) – and thus bore the alleged sin of sexual desire much more heavily than did men. For example, at the beginning of the play – even before Hamlet has encountered the Ghost – he recalls his parents' marriage, focusing not so much on the mutuality of their love for one another as on their incommensurable expressions of it. The chivalrous King Hamlet was 'so loving to my mother' (1.2.140), while the allegedly sexually voracious Gertrude exhibited an 'increase of appetite' (1.2.144) towards her first husband. The Ghost's curious retrospection on what exactly went on in the 'royal bed of Denmark' (1.5.82) supports Hamlet's earlier account of the marriage, which produced only him as its offspring.

King Hamlet's relationship with his wife in the Ghost's account is described as being curiously asexual: the marriage was a matter of 'dignity' and 'virtue'. The image of being 'hand in hand' is used metaphorically and in the period often signified the betrothal ritual of joining hands in the presence of family and friends, which was known as 'handfasting'. Thus, this image intimates the chaste conduct of a couple prior to the consummation of their wedding night, in contrast with the more intensively physical contact implied by 'falling off' to 'decline upon' the 'wretch' Claudius. The Ghost uses personified abstractions to describe his married life, which consist of a bizarre ménage of Virtue, Lewdness, and Lust. In this configuration, Hamlet's father is represented allegorically as Virtue, while Claudius is figured as Lewdness and Gertrude as Lust. Even within the presumably legitimate consummation described here, in which Lust 'Will sate itself', – that is to say, it has achieved sexual gratification in the 'celestial bed' – there is an accusation of sexual voracity against Gertrude. The sexual satisfactions of the celestial bed were apparently not enough for insatiable Lust/Gertrude, who proceeds to hunt for trash, or 'prey on garbage'. The sexual satiation afforded by this connubial intimacy must, then, have been very temporary or entirely deficient. It is, indeed, difficult to imagine that 'a radiant angel' could have had a vigorous sex life. Moreover, 'Virtue' in the above passage is unquestionably linked to sexual continence both within and outside the marriage.

Throughout the play, the friction between Hamlet and his mother is squarely focused on her remarriage. When Rosencrantz and Guildenstern report Gertrude's alarm at Hamlet's behaviour, he announces, apparently with some satisfaction, 'O wonderful son that can so 'stonish a mother!' (3.2.319). Despite professing that he will prove his uncle's perfidy by means of the play-within-the-play, he is vastly more invested in producing evidence of his mother's guilt. The confusion of parental roles caused by Gertrude's remarriage – Claudius becomes Hamlet's 'uncle-father' and Gertrude his 'aunt-mother' (2.2.313) – ignites Hamlet's rather prurient depiction of his mother's sex life:

> In the rank sweat of an enseamed bed
> Stewed in corruption, honeying and making love
> Over the nasty sty –

> (3.4.90–2)

The image is one of filthy and soiled bed linens, but there may also be a sneer at the '[t]hrift, thrift' that, as he joked with Horatio in Act 1, led to 'the funeral baked meats' doing double duty on 'the marriage tables' (1.2.179–80). This is because 'enseamed' (a wonderful word) also refers to the housewifely practice of repairing worn sheets by cutting them down the centre and sewing them up again with the sides to the middle, thereby creating a seam in the centre of the sheet (White, 108). The metre here requires careful examination of the word 'enseamed' because in order to scan it must be pronounced 'enseamèd', with exaggerated emphasis on the final syllable. If we look carefully enough, the line may reveal not what Hamlet alleges – namely, his mother's craven sexual appetite – but, rather antithetically, an interpretation of Gertrude's character as the thrifty good wife who, like Ophelia in her closet, is occupied with the virtuous activities of sewing and mending household linens. Yet, as R. S. White suggests, even these activities may not be viewed by Hamlet as evidence of virtue: 'Recycling, of course, is quite specifically his complaint against his mother for replacing a husband who has been conveniently disposed of, with a second-hand one, a crude job of botching "a king of shreds and patches" (3.4.99) onto the memory of a greater figure' (White, 108). In this potential destabilizing of a word's meaning, we see how Shakespeare allows language to get away from the meanings his characters ostensibly intend in order to reveal more than they might be willing to admit.

Hamlet's tirade against his mother includes not only the charge that she is hypersexual, but also that sexual desire is inappropriate for someone of her age: 'if thou canst mutine in a matron's bones' (3.4.81). Frequently, children of all ages believe that sexual appetite is both impossible and improper for their parents:

> You cannot call it love, for at your age
> The heyday in the blood is tame ...

> (3.4.66–7)

Thompson and Taylor note that male editors have typically assumed that Hamlet is correct in believing that his mother is too old to feel erotic longing, as well as too old to excite it. Yet, as they also note, Gertrude is the same age as Gonzago's wife, 'whose remarriage is viewed with equanimity by her failing husband' (Thompson and Taylor, 341).

An alternative model of widowhood in *Hamlet* is that of the most sympathetic matron in the play, the Trojan Queen Hecuba, wife of Priam, whose extremity of grief after the destruction of Troy eventually turns into madness. Hecuba is a proper object of pity because, as the former Queen of Troy, her crown is now replaced with a head wrap, while a blanket covers the emaciated body that has borne Priam 19 children: '*her lank and all-o'erteemed loins*' (2.2.446). Hers is not the body of a sexually active, mature woman, but rather the body of a pitiably spent, maternal figure.

Widows in Elizabethan England may have remarried for love or also simply in order to have the protection of a husband in a society that did not much favour female autonomy – or perhaps for some admixture of these motives. Nonetheless, Hamlet shares early modern culture's interest in the sex lives of widows, and several plays of the period – both comedies and tragedies – address this theme as well. Most

notably, John Webster's *The Duchess of Malfi* (c. 1612) is
unusually sympathetic to the Duchess's choice of marrying a
second husband, even though she transgresses class boundaries in doing so. Furthermore, Webster's play represents
attempts by the Duchess's brother, Ferdinand, to control his
sister's sexuality as aberrant, motivated by incestuous desire,
and lunatic. (For example, Ferdinand thinks he is a wolf with
hair on the inside.) Although older women also remarried,
sometimes wedding younger men, the Duchess, like many
widows of the period, was still of reproductive age. Much
to the consternation of Queen Mary (Elizabeth's half-sister
and predecessor), for example, Frances Grey, the 40-year-old
Duchess of Suffolk, married her 21-year-old Master of the
Horse, Adrian Stokes, in 1555. Much like Gertrude, she
did so, according to some accounts, only days after her first
husband, Henry Grey, 1st Duke of Suffolk, was executed
for high treason. Frances bore her second husband a child,
although their daughter died in infancy.

One reason for the cultural antipathy towards widows who
remarried was the danger that property, that of the deceased
husband and that belonging to the woman herself, might be
redistributed. Titles also might change hands. For example, if
Gertrude bore Claudius a son, Hamlet would most likely be
disinherited. Gertrude's age is not given, but it may be approxi-
mated from the two indications in the play. First, the Player
King and Queen have been married for 30 years, and secondly,
the Gravedigger says he has been sexton for 30 years, since the
birth of Prince Hamlet. That Hamlet is still at university seems
odd in light of this. Certainly, the impression given early on
in the play is of Hamlet as a young student – a much younger
figure than the apparently 30-year-old he has become by the
Gravediggers' scene in Act 5 scene 1. However, if he were
indeed aged 30, Gertrude would probably have been post-
menopausal and thus incapable of bearing an heir for Claudius,
who might then rival Hamlet as next in line to the throne.

The play-within-the-play offers a further perspective on
the sexual lives of widows. Although the Player King never

explicitly demands a promise from his wife that she not remarry, the Player Queen seems to feel that such an oath is what is required of her: '*Both here and hence pursue me lasting strife / If once I be a widow ever I be a wife*' (3.2.216–17). Shakespeare had addressed the theme of the widow who marries her husband's murderer in his early play, *Richard III* (c. 1592). In a conspicuous departure from historical fact, Richard woos the widowed Anne Neville (quite literally over the dead body of her father-in-law) by telling her he killed her husband because of his passion for her. At least in Hamlet's description, the satyr-like Claudius echoes Richard's physical appearance. Richard was deformed and hunchbacked; he is described as a 'fiend' and a 'hedgehog' (1.2.34; 104) and, ultimately, like Claudius, he murders the widow who has taken him as her second husband.

Despite the Ghost's warning that he must allow Gertrude's conscience 'to prick and sting her' (1.5.88) without any further assistance from him, Hamlet jibes at his mother about her remarriage during the performance of *The Mousetrap*:

| HAMLET | Madam, how like you this play? |
| QUEEN | The lady doth protest too much, methinks. |

(3.2.223–4)

This is not the direct confrontation of the kind that we see in Act 3 scene 4 in Gertrude's chamber, but it is rather a tense moment in a public setting. What is fascinating in this episode, however, is the way in which the play-within-the-play both does and does not mirror events in Elsinore: the murder of Hamlet's father by his uncle and his mother's remarriage to his uncle. Instead, it is Hamlet's theatrical alter ego, 'one Lucianus, nephew to the King' (3.2.237), who is the murderer in this re-enactment. It is he who pours poison into the Player King's ear, and who '*woos the queen with gifts*' (3.2.128:9–10). The Player Queen '*seems harsh awhile but in the end accepts love*' (3.2.128:10–11). Since, by virtue of being the nephew in this scenario, Lucianus in part represents Hamlet himself, there is arguably a repressed incestuous narrative here reminiscent of Hamlet's designation of Gertrude as his 'aunt-mother'. Hamlet earlier joked that the play was called *The Mousetrap*, which is an apt moniker because, of course, he seeks to ensnare Claudius. However, 'mouse' offers another instance of early modern slang for a woman, specifically her female reproductive parts. In *Romeo and Juliet*, for example, Old Capulet is described as having been quite the mouse-hunter in his day (4.4.11). Ostensibly engineered to ensnare Claudius into an admission of guilt, given its lewd early modern meaning, *The Mousetrap* seems to be a disturbingly sexual instrument with which to establish Gertrude's moral culpability as a remarried widow. This is especially the case since Hamlet has rewritten the Ghost's narrative so that the figure that most closely resembles him is one that kills the Player King and seduces the widowed Player Queen. Lucianus, then, both is and is not Hamlet.

Hamlet and Oedipus

Intimations of a submerged, incestuous trajectory of desire in the play led the Freudian critic Ernest Jones to argue in *Hamlet and Oedipus* (1949) that Hamlet, like Sophocles' Oedipus in *Oedipus Rex* (c. 429 BCE), had an *unconscious* desire to kill his father and marry his mother. Jones was a student of Sigmund Freud, the 'father' of psychoanalysis who pioneered the theory that in infancy all human beings wish to possess the mother and eliminate the father who is perceived by the infant as a rival for the mother's love. Importantly, Freud claimed that we do not and cannot remember this phase of our lives. However, the memory of it is not so much forgotten as it is simply repressed, and this distinction is critical. As the infant develops mentally and physically and, with age, becomes more fully integrated into human society, these early desires in relation to the child's parents become unacceptable. In psychosexual terms, the infant is required to repress them, and although these unacceptable desires are no longer present within the conscious mind, they remain hidden in the unconscious memory.

Following Freud's theory, Jones argued that Hamlet cannot kill Claudius because his uncle has done exactly what he himself, albeit unknowingly, or 'unconsciously', had wished to do: namely, to kill his father and copulate with his mother. A comparison of *Hamlet* with *Oedipus Rex* is instructive here. Sophocles' Oedipus does not know that the woman he has married is his mother or that the man he has killed is his father; to Oedipus' horror, this is only subsequently discovered at the play's end. Sophocles' play fascinated Freud, who was interested in how people's desires and motivations were so often unknown even to themselves – unconscious. Freud's theory was appealing in relation to *Hamlet* in part because Hamlet's obsessive interest in his mother's sex life seems to have been motivated by something unrelated to, or at least in excess of, the revenge mission that the Ghost charged him with in Act 1. Indeed, as the play progresses with the *conscious* pursuit of vengeance on his father's behalf, Hamlet's scrutiny of his mother, apparently fuelled by unconscious motivations, only intensifies. The sexual prohibitions Hamlet places upon Gertrude are extraordinary: '[B]y no means ... / Let the bloat King tempt you again to bed' (3.4.179–80).

Whether or not Shakespeare's play proves Freud's theories about human sexuality to be correct, the Oedipal scenario that Jones applied to *Hamlet* was persuasive particularly because of its intersection with the play's focus on memory. When, in his first soliloquy, Hamlet unleashes his misogynistic accusation, 'Frailty, thy name is Woman' (1.2.146), he also pronounces the urgent wish to forget: '(Let me not think on't' (1.2.146), ultimately asking himself, 'Must I remember?' (1.2.143).

Further, the suppressed Catholic practice of building chantries, ''a must build churches' (3.2.126) prefaces the play-within-the-play. Chantries were dedicated to remembering the dead, and especially to praying for the 'holy souls' in Purgatory. Because the law forbade it after the Protestant Reformation, this was a practice that all Elizabethans were required to 'forget'. Indeed, Hamlet rehearses the need both to remember and to forget the dead and considers the important distinction between honouring the memory of the departed and keeping their grievances alive. The play is consumed with acts of remembering and forgetting that constitute personal and cultural memory. From the opening scenes, where Hamlet is indicted by Claudius and his mother for excessive mourning, to the Gravediggers' scene, the theme of memory persists as one of the key dynamics of revenge tragedy. The dead in the play, like the bodily remains in the graveyard, are at once anonymous heaps of bones and vivid reminders of particular individuals, such as the jester, Yorick, whose comedy was 'wont to set / the table on a roar' (5.1.180–1).

The double standard

When Rosencrantz and Guildenstern want to establish their friendship with Hamlet in order to pry information from him, their attempt at male bonding takes the form of ribaldry, and their banter is peppered with slightly off-colour, sexual jokes. In this case, the jokes are not about Gertrude's body but about that of the Roman goddess, Fortuna:

GUILDENSTERN
   On Fortune's cap we are not the very button.
HAMLET   Nor the soles of her shoe.
ROSENCRANTZ   Neither, my lord.
HAMLET   Then you live about her waist, or in the
   middle of her favours.
GUILDENSTERN   Faith, her privates we.
HAMLET   In the secret parts of Fortune? O, most true
   – she is a strumpet.

(2.2.224–31)

The visitors' fortunes are middling, neither on the top nor the bottom. The dirty joke is that they are Fortune's intimates – 'her privates' – an idea that Hamlet elaborates on to say that they have penetrated her private parts, her genitalia, because she is a whore, or 'a strumpet'. This is a cultural commonplace in the period that Shakespeare uses elsewhere, as, for example, when the Fool says in *King Lear*, 'Fortune, that arrant whore' (2.4.51) (Greenblatt, *Norton*, et al.). Here, far from discovering misogyny as a language he has in common with Rosencrantz and Guildenstern, as Thompson and Taylor suggest in their note on the passage, Hamlet may be suggesting that his erstwhile school friends have prostituted themselves to the king (54).

The most reviled of women in early modern England, prostitutes, were also held accountable for luring men from virtue. Men themselves bore little or none of the blame if they took advantage of their services. Thus, visiting prostitutes, or 'drabbing' (2.1.26), according to Polonius, is par for the course for a young man away at university, one of 'such wanton, wild and usual slips / As are companions noted and most known / To youth and liberty' (2.1.22–4). This double standard is emphasized even more by the strict control maintained over aristocratic young women like Ophelia. She is lectured by both her father and her brother about the dangers of opening her 'chaste treasure' (1.3.30) and urged repeatedly that her 'best safety lies in fear' (1.2.42).

Ophelia counters Laertes' pious disquisition on her chastity with a reminder that he should not play the hypocrite. This is a remarkable moment in the play from the point of view of gender dynamics, a moment during which Ophelia displays a sense of humour and a capacity to mock her brother's pious pronouncements. In what is undoubtedly prescient advice, since her father expects her brother to be visiting brothels in Paris, she also asserts that sexual continence should apply as much to men as it does to women:

I shall the effect of this good lesson keep
As watchman to my heart. But, good my brother,

> Do not as some ungracious pastors do
> Show me the steep and thorny way to heaven
> Whiles, a puffed and reckless libertine,
> Himself the primrose path of dalliance treads
> And recks not his own rede.

$$(1.3.44-9)$$

Ophelia succeeds in maintaining a balance in her duty as a chaste and obedient sister who attends her brother's warnings without becoming devoid of will or personality. Situating her brother's lecture within the realm of religious discourse, she remarks on the 'good lesson', a term also used in early modern English church services where scriptural readings concluded with, 'Here endeth the lesson.' Ophelia's repetition of 'good' almost subliminally associates her with goodness and chaste submission. 'Grace', too, is a key word in Protestantism because when the German reformer, Martin Luther, formulated his theses, which he famously nailed to the door of the parish church in Wittenberg, one of the most controversial of them, and the one which most sharply divided Protestants from Catholics, was the doctrine that salvation was the result of *sola gratia*, or 'grace alone'. The image of clergy not thus endowed with grace – '*ungracious* pastors' – has the residual effect of summoning up a vision of pre-Reformation Catholic clerics, some of whose abuses (prominent among them, sexual impropriety) had led directly to the institution of the reformed religion.

'[T]he steep and thorny way to heaven' was another traditional Christian precept that maintained that the path to salvation was not easy, but rather narrow and difficult, while the road to hell was wide – an eight-lane highway with no traffic. There are a number of contemporary illustrations in which robed clerics are depicted as heading down a wide path, oblivious to the fact that the mouth of hell awaits them at its end. In one engraving from a drawing by Bernard Van Orley (c. 1550), titled 'Love not the World, neither the things that are in the world' (1 John 2.15), a papal tiara sits on the top of the hell mouth that is devouring the hypocritical churchman. However, 'thorny' is also a scriptural word from the parable of the sower in St. Mark's Gospel, which explains why some people who hear the word of God, which is described as seed, do not absorb it: 'And some fell among the thorns, and the thorns grew up, and choked it, so that it gave no fruit' (Mk 4.7). These scriptural references had become proverbial wisdom by Shakespeare's time. The 'primrose path' was the commonplace term for a life whose philosophy was devoted to sensual enjoyment, or, as St. Paul summarized it: 'Let us eat and drink for tomorrow we shall die' (1 Cor. 15.32). It becomes very clear from Ophelia's biblical references that she knows the scripture very well, and indeed her speech far outdoes her brother's as an expression of piety. Where Ophelia's language becomes distinctively original, however, is when she warns Laertes not to become 'a puffed and reckless libertine'. The libertine was a distinctively masculine figure – one who is promiscuous, amoral and heedless of the consequences of his actions. In the eighteenth century, the character of the libertine became a popular literary type.

That Ophelia has absorbed the Word of God like a good Christian is important because women's speech, conventionally associated with unchastity and disobedience, was always a double-edged sword. In this passage Shakespeare deploys the common store of scriptural and proverbial language to craft a portrait of Ophelia as a chaste, obedient, yet intelligent and perceptive character. This is always a danger with wholly virtuous characters in literature – that, being devoid of flaws and failings, they will therefore lack anything to mark their distinctive particularities as characters.

'[L]ike a whore' (2.2.520)

Given the cultural antipathy towards prostitutes, as well as the pressure on women to conform to a very restricted understanding of virtue, it is somewhat surprising that, at times, Hamlet regards himself as a whore. In the soliloquy beginning with the **apostrophe** (or abstract address), 'O, what a rogue and peasant slave am I!' (2.2.485), the crescendo in this litany of self-recrimination is the figure of the 'drab':

> Why, what an ass am I: this is most brave,
> That I, the son of a dear murdered,
> Prompted to my revenge by heaven and hell,
> Must like a whore unpack my heart with words
> And fall a-cursing like a very drab ...

> (2.2.517–21)

Why do words make Hamlet a whore? Why are they such a pronounced aspect of Hamlet's ostensible femininity? Patricia Parker argues:

> In the traditional opposition of genders in which 'Women are words, men deeds,' Hamlet's comparison of his verbal and deedless delay to the impotent anger of a drab sets up a link between his entire period of inactivity and delay and womanish wordiness, in contrast to such one-dimensional emblems of masculinity as Laertes and the aptly named Fort-in-bras [strong-in-arms] (qtd. in Thompson and Taylor, 277).

When Hamlet becomes a whore he is at the nadir of self-loathing, although as Kay Stanton remarks, it is curious that 'Hamlet compares his *in*ability to kill his current king with behaving like a "whore"' (Stanton, 25). This is not an illustration of 'other folks' whoring', suggested by D. H. Lawrence, or even 'whoring' in the sense of visiting prostitutes; rather, this is Hamlet assuming the identity of a whore. Here, language – 'words' – and even envenomed forms of speech such as imprecations, or 'cursing', become the antithesis of power. Further, the metaphor of a heart full of words that can only be 'unpacked' and spoken by the prostitute works to denigrate language itself as feminine.

That Hamlet is both a son *and* a whore in the above passage is a somewhat astonishing juxtaposition of qualities. Here, notably, Hamlet is his father's son, but 'whore' implicitly aligns him with his mother, and this is a relationship he wishes to disavow: 'And, would it were not so, you are my mother' (3.4.15). We noted the striking dissimilarity that Hamlet emphasizes between himself and his Herculean father in the previous chapter. If Hamlet is not like his father, he is, then, arguably like his mother. Certainly, in his identification with degraded womanhood, there are intimations of maternal resemblance. That is, when Hamlet declares he is like a woman, like a whore, the woman he is most likely to resemble is his mother. Shakespeare writes of the beautiful young man in Sonnet 3 who so closely resembles his mother: 'Thou art thy mother's glass, and she in thee / Calls back the lovely April of her prime' (*l.* 9–10). In this instance, mother and son are almost mirror images of one another, and while there is no sense of such direct, physical resemblance between Gertrude and Hamlet, their relationship is described by Claudius in terms of their having parallel, mirrored lives: 'The Queen his mother / Lives almost by his looks' (4.7.12–13). That is, Gertrude is dependent upon how Hamlet looks – sad, thoughtful and melancholic – for her own well-being, and even for her life.

Violence against women: 'words like daggers' (3.4.92)

When Hamlet expostulates with his mother in the intimate space of her 'closet' (her bedchamber or other private room) he uses language as an instrument of violence. This is studied, but not retributive, violence; Hamlet's goal here is not payback. However, Hamlet's rage towards his mother creates the conditions for a sudden, violent and unpremeditated 'rash and bloody deed' (3.4.25) – the murder of Polonius:

> Soft, now to my mother.
> O heart, lose not thy nature. Let not ever
> The soul of Nero enter this firm bosom –
> Let me be cruel, not unnatural:
> I will speak daggers to her but use none.
> My tongue and soul in this be hypocrites.
> How in my words somever she be shent
> To give them seals never my soul consent.
>
> (3.2.382–9)

Particularly disturbing here is the reference to the Roman emperor Nero who not only famously committed matricide, but also ripped out his mother's womb. Hamlet is careful *not* to be like him: 'I will speak daggers to her, but use none.' This line can be taken to mean that Hamlet understands that, given the ferocity of the address he intends to deliver to his mother, using actual weapons against her would simply be redundant. This is the opposite of Romeo's assertion that he would rend his own name if he could, rather than be the enemy of his beloved Juliet: 'Had I it written, I would tear the word' (2.2.57).

Hamlet, however, succeeds in doing violence with his knife of words: 'O Hamlet, thou hast cleft my heart in twain' (3.4.154). Again, in Act 5 Hamlet has physical aggression against women on his mind. Arguably, he takes some delight in imagining a woman's jawless skull being 'knocked about': '[M]y Lady Worm's – chapless and knocked about the mazard with a sexton's spade' (5.1.83–5). Words can, indeed, perpetrate violence but, as when Romeo speaks of rending his name, violence can be done to words. However, in *Hamlet* the emphasis is on the destructive powers of language, specifically when used against women.

Ophelia: 'Her speech is nothing' (4.5.7)

In the wake of his father's murder, Hamlet finds femininity reprehensible, both the ways women carry themselves and the ways they speak: 'You jig and amble and you lisp, you / nickname God's creatures' (3.1.143–4). The idea that women lisp refers to the affectation of speaking childishly and is of a piece with the charge that women nickname animals. Adam named the animals in the book of Genesis. Women, according to Hamlet, rename them and are thus implicitly indicted for usurping the male prerogative in relation to language rather than for merely misusing it. Only after Ophelia loses her senses does her language become disordered, at least by the measure of the patriarchal logic of the court. Hamlet's earlier point, however, appears to be that women with their alleged jigging and ambling are themselves an impediment to all forms of bodily decorum, especially that of speech.

There is, however, no instance in *Hamlet* in which a female character uses a nickname for an animal. Rather, in her mesmerizing elegy for Ophelia, Gertrude reports that both men and women rename natural objects. Young men give rude names to phallic flowers, while virgins, or 'cold maids', use euphemisms for them: 'dead men's fingers' (4.7.169). This nomenclature, far from being some courtly affectation, which is the gist of Hamlet's accusation, is in fact a return to the natural world and to a sexuality that is less guarded by spying parents and rigid codes of feminine conduct than it is at court. Gertrude's pastoral description is, indeed, the very antithesis of the starched, repressive world that confined Ophelia:

> There is a willow grows askant the brook
> That shows his hoary leaves in the glassy stream.
> Therewith fantastic garlands did she make
> Of crowflowers, nettles, daisies and long purples,
> That liberal shepherds give a grosser name
> But our cold maids do dead men's fingers call them.

There on the pendent boughs her crownet weeds
Clambering to hang, an envious sliver broke,
When down her weedy trophies and herself
Fell in the weeping brook. Her clothes spread wide
And mermaid-like awhile they bore her up,
Which time she chanted snatches of old lauds
As one incapable of her own distress,
Or like a creature native and endued
Unto that element. But long it could not be
Till that her garments, heavy with their drink,
Pulled the poor wretch from her melodious lay
To muddy death.

(4.7.164–81)

The dead are littered throughout this pastoral landscape:
'cold maids' are literally chaste girls who refrain from obscene
language, but 'cold' also connotes now-dead virgins who had
named the flowers as 'dead men's fingers'. The flowers Ophelia
decks herself with are not only blossoms but also brief lyrical
phrases known as 'flowers' or 'poesies', and her death is a
kind of mythical transformation from maid to mermaid in
a metamorphosis that continues until she becomes indistin-
guishable from the watery landscape itself. Gertrude, then,
seems to be able to speak about human sexuality without
making it seem unnatural – the '*liberal* shepherds' are young
men who use uncouth language and who are, in Gertrude's
speech, brought into conversation with those 'cold maids'.
There is a kind of wooing dance going on throughout the lines.
Ophelia, too, is described not only in virginal imagery but also
in relation to sexual knowledge and experience through the
image of the 'hoary' leaves of the weeping willow tree, which
is given a male pronoun: '*his* hoary leaves'. In the Folio, the
word is 'hoar', but in both cases, the word is a homonym for
'whore'. Shakespeare uses this wordplay in a similar fashion
in *Romeo and Juliet* (2.4.106), but in *Hamlet* the 'hoar'
refers to the natural bristliness of foliage, and it is only if we

attend to this carefully that we hear in the passage the echo and distillation of all that Hamlet said earlier about Gertrude and Ophelia: 'whore'. When, at the end of the speech, we arrive at the sexually charged description of Ophelia with 'Her clothes spread wide', and thus of the undoing of all the sexual restraint that has been socially imposed on her, we are left with the sense of what R. S. White has called 'the lateral inclusiveness' of Gertrude's imagery. Gertrude, as he explains, 'comments through empathy on the young woman's capacity for ... innocence and a "grosser" knowingness about sexual matters. At least part of the tragedy for both Ophelia and Gertrude is their gender solitude and separation from each other' (White, 110).

There is only one direct and poignant conversation between the two women, which occurs just as Claudius dismisses Gertrude in Act 3 scene 3, at which point she addresses Ophelia directly. Here, in contrast to Polonius and Laertes, both of whom tell Ophelia that 'Lord Hamlet is a prince out of thy star' (2.2.138), Gertrude seems to view a marriage between Hamlet and Ophelia as a desirable and as an imminent possibility:

QUEEN
    And for your part, Ophelia, I do wish
    That your good beauties be the happy cause
    Of Hamlet's wildness. So shall I hope your virtues
    Will bring him to his wonted way again
    To both your honours.
OPHELIA   Madam, I wish it may.

                        (3.1.36–40)

Gertrude's account of the death of Ophelia (4.7) is her longest speech in the play, and like Ophelia's longest speech (her report of Hamlet's visit to her 'closet') it is also a reported scene, or 'unscene'. This is the difference between showing, **mimesis**, and telling, **diegesis**. Diegesis achieves a distinctive, almost emblematic theatrical effect since it is what early moderns would have called 'a speaking picture' (Karim-Cooper, 222). In Ophelia's speech, Hamlet is figured as the emblem of the melancholic lover, and in Gertrude's, Ophelia is the emblem, to borrow Laertes' earlier phrase, of the now dying 'rose of May', (4.5.156). These reported episodes also create a temporal depth within the narrative of the play because they refer to what happened while the audience or reader was attending to other things. Such passages can also serve as a form of what we might call textual unconsciousness – that is, they refer to elements such as deep emotions that are beneath the surface of the linear plot.

Hamlet has accused Ophelia of sexual immorality and ordered her no fewer than five times to 'Get thee to a nunnery!' (3.1.120). Since 'nunnery' is both a convent and, in early modern slang, the term for a brothel, it is perhaps unsurprising that sexual language surfaces in Ophelia's speech as her rational faculties recede. Her language abdicates entirely the practical purposes of communication and 'ascends' to lyrical associativeness as she rehearses ballads, hymns and bawdy rhymes. Hers is a potent language which is characterized at times by unnervingly candid sexual desire and, at others by stark emotional need:

> They bore him bare-faced on the bier
> > And in his grave rained many a tear.
> Fare you well, my dove.

> (4.5.160–2)

This poignant image of a coffinless corpse and his grieving mourners implies a story, but it does not possess a linear narrative structure, and in this its power lies. The final, doleful line suggests that the bereaved singer mourns her dead lover rather than, as Ophelia does, a dead parent. However, she has also lost Hamlet, even though he remains alive.

Nothing

The play as a whole, but especially Hamlet himself, obsesses over the woman's 'nothing' – that is, in Elizabethan slang, the vagina, because there is no 'thing' (penis). Hamlet's famous pun on 'country matters' (3.2.110), or 'cunt' – that is, the 'fair thought' that lies 'between maids' legs' (3.2.112) makes this clear. However, Hamlet also seems to be considering what women signify in the corrupt patriarchal court of Elsinore. Laertes, who does not suffer from Hamlet's gender trouble, can say of his sister's speech, 'This nothing's more than matter' (4.5.168), thus ceding priority to women's language over the rational, coherent language of the patriarchal court. In contrast, Hamlet seems to want to keep control over women's speech. For instance, he finds it imponderable that the Player can work himself into a passion for the sake of the widowed Queen of Troy, who is also a 'nothing':

> and all for nothing –
> For Hecuba?
> What's Hecuba to him, or he to her,
> That he should weep for her?

> (2.2.492–5)

The tragedy of Hamlet is that he cannot weep for his own 'Wretched Queen' (5.2.317).

'The woman will be out' (4.7.187)

'The woman will be out' is how Laertes describes the moment when he will be able to stop weeping for his sister's death. Such ostensibly feminine emotions are, as Laertes admits, a source of shame that should be purged from the body. This idea was not only a metaphor, it was also an established aspect of one of the dominant medical theories of the time derived from the treatises of the classical physician, Galen. The idea that the woman will be 'out' implies both the excise of emotion and the sense that its display is inherently feminine. Laertes' masculinity and his role as the courtier-avenger thus require the refusal of tears.

This makes for a marked contrast with Hamlet who, while he is neither considered feminine in the world of the play nor would he have been considered effeminate in Elizabethan England, has been, since the late eighteenth century, firmly associated with femininity. This is surprising insofar as he is the vehicle for the play's most virulent misogyny. However, the idea of a feminine Hamlet arises from the Romantic view of his oversensitive nature and his vacillation. After all, 'To be or not to be' could be understood not as a profound philosophical inquiry but rather as a case of terminal indecision. Hamlet has often been performed, as Thompson and Taylor observe, as 'sensitive, oppressed' and 'paralysed by consciousness' (103). However, Hamlet's ostensibly feminine side was not always viewed as a negative dimension of his character. For example, the American actor (and, as we have seen, the brother of Abraham Lincoln's assassin), Edwin Booth, sought to stress Hamlet's intellectual and spiritual qualities, which he associated with women. He wrote in 1882 that he had 'always endeavoured to make prominent the femininity of Hamlet's character' (Thompson and Taylor, 103). The interpretation of Hamlet as intrinsically feminine led to a stage tradition of women playing Hamlet. The great actress Sarah Siddons was the first woman to play Hamlet in 1775, and female Hamlets continued to be popular through the nineteenth century. In addition to Siddons, famous female performers included Kitty Clive, Charlotte Cushman, Julia Glover and, most famous of all, Sarah Bernhardt. However, there have been women Hamlets in the twentieth century, too – including Eva Le Gallienne and the 73-year-old Judith Anderson. This tradition has not, however, been universally applauded, as W. H. Auden's vindictive remark makes clear: 'Curiously, everyone tries to identify with Hamlet, even actresses – and in fact

Sarah Bernhardt did play Hamlet, and I am glad to say she broke her leg in doing it' (Auden, 159).

Male bonding

Since royal courts in early modern Europe were associated with refinement and civility, neither Hamlet nor Laertes conform to a model of warrior masculinity. However, Hamlet's relationship with Horatio fits the period's ideal of friendship, which was, unsurprisingly, between men:

> Since my dear soul was mistress of her choice
> And could of men distinguish her election
> Sh'ath sealed thee for herself.

> (3.2.59–61)

Since Hamlet was old enough to have powers of discernment, he has chosen Horatio as his best friend forever. The soul, or *anima*, is always feminine, and it is that feminine, most interior aspect of Hamlet – that 'which passes show' (1.2.85) – that so cherishes Horatio's friendship. That their friendship is 'sealed' suggests a relationship that is analogous to the conjugal bond and the indissoluble ties of matrimony, and certainly a much closer connection than that between Hamlet and Ophelia. The quasi-homoerotic dimension of their friendship was not at all unusual in the period, which possessed neither our own rigid distinctions of sexual identity nor any hesitance about using erotic language to express same-sex bonds. This sealing of their friendship also anticipates the legal authority Hamlet assumes when he uses his father's signet ring with the Danish seal to emend the documents being sent from Claudius to the English King. Bonds between men in this play can be sealed, whereas ties with the play's women are abrogated and broken.

While there have been many noteworthy performances of Hamlet by both women and men, one that is especially pertinent to the relationship between Hamlet and Horatio is the silent film made in Germany in 1920, *Hamlet: the Drama of Vengeance*, directed by Svend Gade and Heinz Schall and starring the glamorous female Danish movie star, Asta Nielson, as Hamlet. In this version, Hamlet is discovered to be a woman by the accidental uncovering of 'his' bosom in the final duel. Embracing Hamlet, Horatio touches 'her' breast and declares that he now understands what drew him to Hamlet: 'Death reveals thy tragic secret. Now I understand what bound me to that matchless form and feature – Your true heart was a woman's. Too late – beloved – 'tis too late' (Howard, 54). As he kisses Hamlet, a homoerotic attraction is conveniently converted into a heterosexual one. This adaptation was inspired by the late nineteenth-century critic E. P. Vining's ingenious (and hilarious) thesis – built without any foundation on Shakespeare's text – that Hamlet was actually a woman and disguised only to preserve patrilineal inheritance. While this may seem outlandish, both Vining's thesis and the film nonetheless drew on a long tradition that understood Hamlet as a feminized tragic hero.

Review

We have now covered a range of issues that relate to the ways language creates character in *Hamlet*, and we have seen how understandings of character change through time. We have also examined the ways in which various dimensions of Hamlet's character are developed in relation to the political predicament he confronts in Elsinore and through his relationships with the play's women.

Writing matters

1 Choose no more than ten lines from the play and perform a close analysis of them. Write continuously for twenty minutes. While you may want to say where these lines occur in relation to the play's narrative as a whole, be careful not to get caught up in rehearsing the plot; rather, make sure that everything you say about the lines is clearly related to this one passage. At first, you may think you can't find enough to say about such a small amount of text, but you will probably find that once you get going, you have much more to say than time allows. I suggest that you begin by rereading your passage and brainstorming ideas.

2 Explain how your passage analysis relates to the play as a whole, but again, without retelling the plot. What you are learning to do here, first, is how to move in for a close analysis and then how to step back and put that analysis within the big picture of interpretation.

3 Reread W. H. Auden's comments about Ophelia. Then, argue against him or support his argument. Since the exercise is about developing a strong interpretative line, there can be no fence-sitting on this one – you need to pick a side and then marshal all the textual evidence you can in defence of it.

CHAPTER FOUR

Writing an essay: 'Mark the play' (3.2.140–1)

After the dumb show, Ophelia asks Hamlet, 'What means this, my lord?' (3.2.129). It is one of the most forthright questions of the play. Hamlet's response is cryptic: 'It means mischief' (3.2.130–1). In the courtly audience of Elsinore, Ophelia appears to be something of a naïve spectator. She believes that there must be a plausible explanation for the baffling change of erotic direction on the part of the Player Queen. Ophelia wants the early modern equivalent of a plot summary, 'the argument', and some way to get her bearings: 'Belike this show imports the argument of the / play' (3.2.132–3). When the Player enters, Ophelia asks again, 'Will 'a tell us what this show meant?' (3.2.136). She is right to be perplexed: she does not know that King Hamlet was murdered, or that a ghost appeared to Hamlet, so she has absolutely no context for making sense of what she has seen. No one, of course, is going to tell her what the show meant, and Hamlet, in a fit of raging misogyny, makes an obscene jest toward a game of 'show and tell' – if she'll show her genitals, the Player will tell her what they mean (what their respective functions are) or, perhaps, what their exhibition means (an invitation to sex). Having done her best to be patient with him, an exasperated Ophelia turns her attention towards the play: 'You are naught, you are naught. I'll mark the / play' (3.2.140–1).

I find myself identifying with Ophelia here, and you may too. We want to know what the play means, what it imports, but the riddling responses with which the play greets our inquiries are sometimes frustrating. On this particular occasion, however, we know much more than Ophelia. We know more about what the show meant although we still do not know why Lucianus is the murdering nephew to the king when, if art mirrored life in Elsinore, he would, by rights, be the king's brother. However, when Ophelia asks about the import of the show we also have the sense that even if Hamlet were to give her the facts straight, with no riddles or lewd *double entendres*, there would still be an awful lot of meaning left out. This is because from the tragic point of view, there is something ungraspable – something unknowable about the human condition and about, especially in the face of evil, whether it has any meaning at all. Tragedy shows us that pat answers won't do. What is important, as *Hamlet* demonstrates time and time again, is the critical calibre of the questions we ask.

Ophelia is almost a stand-in for all of us – the play's readers and for the audience at the court of Elsinore who have witnessed the dumb show – but her questions are of a much narrower range than those posed by Hamlet. She's hoping to pin the show down, to contain its meaning and evaporate its mystery once and for all. Tragedy, especially one as dense and complex as *Hamlet*, does not allow for that. What I admire about Ophelia, however, is the way she reacts in the face of Hamlet's refusal to explain the show. She turns to the play in front of her and says, 'I'll mark the play.' 'Mark' conveys more than, for instance, 'I'll watch the play.' It suggests, rather, the kind of concentrated attention required to derive meaning from our own perspectives without the guidance or interpretations of others. Ultimately, no one else – either in your life or in your Shakespeare course – can produce meaning for you. It's something we simply have to do for ourselves. Like Ophelia, all that we can do in the face of textual inscrutability is to turn again and again and again to the text and literally 'mark the play'.

From Shakespeare's writing to your own

The exercises in this book so far have been designed to develop the critical thinking skills necessary for writing a full-length paper. In particular, the ways that you have been learning to hone in on particular sections of the text and to read the features of its language in close detail are crucial to writing a successful essay. Now, unless you have been given a very specific topic, you need to decide what, exactly, you are going to write about. If your instructor or examiner has given you a topic, you will need to decide how to narrow your focus and how to use textual evidence to best explore and analyse the issue or question that has been posed to you. First of all, don't sit down with a blank sheet of paper. Sit down with the play itself and with your notes, and make sure you re-read the play before you even consider drafting the paper. When you put pen to paper, recall that you are in exactly the same situation as Shakespeare was in 1600 – paper, writing instrument and then a series of decisions about what word, idea, or detail goes where and how to best phrase and organize your thoughts.

As you reread the play, review your notes and look over the series of exercises you completed earlier, you will begin to develop more specific ideas for your paper. Write down as many as you can. The more ideas you can generate, the more likely you are to come up with a viable topic. Brainstorm! The so-called terror of the blank page will greatly diminish once you have scrawled all over it. Put bookmarks in the passages of the play that have really captured your attention, and take notes on why it is that these particular passages have appealed to you. This process will help you decide later which parts of the text will work best as evidence to support your argument.

Selecting a topic

As you consider how you might focus your paper, you will
no doubt have to engage with some of the questions that
readers have long asked about the play: Did Gertrude commit
adultery with Claudius? Did she conspire with him to have
her husband murdered? Did Hamlet and Ophelia ever sleep
together? While *Hamlet* may invite these sorts of queries, the
play provides us with no clear answers to them – and neither
can you. These questions cannot be definitively answered
because they ask about characters whose existence is confined
to the text of the play. If the text does not provide the answer
to a question, then any answer you produce will be purely
speculative. This does not mean, of course, that you are
wrong to have even considered, say, the nature and extent of
Hamlet and Ophelia's courtship, or the precise nature of the
transgressions that Gertrude feels pangs of guilt about after
Hamlet harangues her in her closet. (Potential sources of her
renewed remorse include remarriage, incest, adultery, and
conspiracy in her husband's murder.) Instead of suppressing
your intrigue about such matters, transform your questions
into viable avenues of inquiry. One way to do this is to go
back to the play and find the parts of the text that excited these
questions in the first place, scouring the play for evidence that
may help you. For example, in Q2, we can make no definitive
determination about Gertrude's sexual behaviour, but Q1,
in which Gertrude is explicit about her ignorance of the
murder, presents (quite literally) a different story altogether.
Even without Q1, you might want to think about Gertrude's
predicament as the widowed mother of a 30-year-old man
and whether or to what degree an early modern audience
might approve or disapprove of her remarriage. What clues in
the play help guide you toward an answer to this question? If
you believe that the audience is, indeed, meant to disapprove
of Gertrude's remarriage, then you'll next need to determine
whether the object of this disapproval is based primarily

on the fact that Gertrude remarried at all or, whether it is because she did so with such unseemly haste, or whether it is because she married her brother-in-law.

As for the question of whether or not Hamlet and Ophelia have had a sexual relationship, a better angle from which to approach this matter would be to explore the details of their relationship that are provided by the play. By doing so, we gravitate back towards the text itself. If you are writing a research paper, you might examine historical accounts of courtship in the period, or you could analyse how film and television adaptations of *Hamlet* have or have not dealt with this issue. Kenneth Branagh's *Hamlet* (1996), for example, inserts a steamy love scene to suggest the seriousness and intensity of Hamlet's relationship with Ophelia, the woman he ultimately rejects. You can thus transform questions such as these that often appear at the outset to have 'yes' or 'no' answers into workable arguments about some of the play's major thematic issues.

You might also consider how you might respond to some favourite questions about the play, such as the old chestnut, why does Hamlet delay? Has Shakespeare deliberately chosen the path of ambiguity here? Or is it that this is simply the wrong kind of question to ask – one that does not consider Hamlet's ethical trepidation about murder?

The argument

The most important feature of your essay aside from the quality of the writing is the argument. By this I do not mean that you need to pick a fight with someone, such as your instructor or a critic whose work you have read. You *could* do this if, for example, you have very strong opinions on a particular topic, but for the most part, an argument in this context simply means that you will be articulating your stated perspective on the play.

After you have assembled all your notes and earlier writing exercises, you may have a better sense of where you want to go with your essay, but it is highly unlikely that you will have a full-fledged argument in place. What you should be able to come up with at this stage is a statement of purpose – what you intend to focus on, as well as some idea of the direction toward which you think your interests tend. Then, make a rough outline of your paper – a sense of the basic structure and parts of the play that you will be using as evidence.

Eventually, your argument will need a clear and coherent thesis statement, but this will only develop as you start writing and rewriting. The thesis statement – the clear and concise articulation of the argument of the paper – will get sharper and tighter as your ideas progress. The thesis statement is the keystone of your paper, and you will need to keep returning to it throughout the writing process.

It is important, too, not to preface your argument with statements such as 'In my opinion'. It is already clear that the argument of the paper belongs to you because the paper has your name on it. Also, simply because there are multiple instances of something – animal imagery, for example – doesn't necessarily mean that it's important within the context of your particular take on the play. You will need to make the case for the significance of animal imagery and illustrate how and why it is important to understanding the play as a whole.

It is also important to remember that you do not need to put your argument at the very beginning of the paper. In fact, it's usually better if you don't and that you spend a paragraph, or at least a few sentences, introducing your idea. Then, be sure to develop it. There is nothing more annoying, from an instructor's or examiner's point of view, than to read a student's introduction and then to read it again in the second paragraph. This is why your plan is so important. The plan is not set in stone, but it will stop you from saying the same thing over and over again. You can always modify the plan in the details, but you should stick to it firmly in terms of the overall direction of the essay. This discipline will stop you from getting stuck midway and will keep your argument rolling along.

After you have clearly articulated your thesis – your controlling idea – you will need to elaborate on it. One of the most important ways of doing this is to, once again, turn back to the text and examine it in detail to support your points. This is where all those exercises we did earlier start to pay big dividends. As a reminder, the goal of the exercises was to help you write fluently – to encourage you to think outside the box about *Hamlet*, and to allow you to move away from vague generalizations towards more concrete, specific practices of textual analysis.

Your thesis statement

This is where you state the argument of your paper. In order to make your thesis really clear and powerful, you will need to keep going over it as you draft and redraft your paper. The thesis is, if you like, your paper in a nutshell. Students often fall into the trap of spending a long time thinking up an ingenious title for their papers – something snazzy – yet, in turn, they end up spending very little time on the actual thesis statement. Thinking about a title can be a way of doing what your thesis is meant to do, namely to provide a microcosm of your paper's argument. However, there are no exam points or essay points for titles, so do not waste too much time on them. Think instead about how you can apply the brainpower you would have spent thinking up a clever title to your paper's thesis statement, which is longer and more expansive. There is more room in a thesis statement for subtlety and nuance, for finer calibration, than there is in a title. Also, a thesis demands that everything in the paper be subordinate to it, whereas a title floats at the top of the first page without the same need to secure solid connections between one idea and another, or between the full range of the essay's ideas and the central argument of the paper.

Once you have the thesis, you must make sure that absolutely everything in your essay refers back to it. Your argument can be quite complex and can even allow for contradiction, and as long as your thesis is clear, you are free to explore these complexities and offer insight into how they bear on your overall argument.

Research

If you are a beginning student, your research will be confined mainly to the text itself, to this book and to the Thompson and Taylor introduction to the play. Do not dismiss these steps or assume that they do not apply to you. Even very experienced Shakespeare scholars begin their writing projects with the text and the editorial introduction and spend a great deal of time with them. I urge you to do the same. There is a wealth of material in your edition of *Hamlet*, and one of the best things you can do for your writing is to learn to take full advantage of it. Remember too that the play text itself is much, much more than just a starting point. Rather, it constitutes the entire focus of your writing project and you will need to work closely with it at every stage.

The whole point of writing a paper is to discover what you think about the play, to investigate it, not to regurgitate someone else's ideas. After your introductory Shakespeare course, you may well want to explore secondary sources and the critical literature that has grown up around *Hamlet*, but once you do that, you will be reading what other critics have to say about the play with the same sophistication with which you have learned to read the text. In other words, you will really be entering into conversation with other writers about the play, rather than simply swallowing whole everything they have said.

There are some very useful sources on the Internet. In particular, I recommend YouTube videos of performances of the play. I have listed some *bona fide* electronic resources below, but do be wary of Internet sources. There's a lot of rubbish out there, and if you are interested in a particular Shakespeare website, it is probably best to check it out first with your instructor or a librarian. A good rule of thumb is to use electronic sources that are available through your own university library.

That said, electronic research can be a huge distraction from job one, which is to read the text carefully, repeatedly and from there, to work towards framing your essay.

Why are you doing this?

I noted at the start of this book that what you and your generation have to say about *Hamlet* will make an important contribution to a conversation that has been going on for several centuries. When Hamlet insists that Horatio survive to 'tell my story', he does so because he knows that the ending of tragedy isn't the act of dying, but the act of telling, and then retelling, the tragic predicament the play presents not just through performance but also through criticism and interpretation. This process defines the cultural work of tragedy, whose imperative is to tell the story, to engage with its language and to consider what can be learned from *Hamlet* in the present. However, this is also your task, to tell the play's story equipped with the critical skills you have learnt from your classes and from this book. In accomplishing it with commitment, you can make a unique and powerful contribution to the cultures and communities we all inhabit.

BIBLIOGRAPHY AND FURTHER READING

Adelman, Janet. *Suffocating Mothers: Fantasies of Maternal Origin in Shakespeare's Plays, Hamlet to The Tempest.* New York: Routledge, 1992.

Aeschylus. *The Oresteia.* Trans. Robert Fagles. New York: Penguin, 1979.

Alexander, Catherine M. S., ed. *Shakespeare and Language.* Cambridge: Cambridge University Press, 2004.

Alexander, Gavin, ed. *Sidney's 'The Defence of Poesy' and Selected Renaissance Literary Criticism.* New York: Penguin, 2004.

Aristotle, *'Poetics,' Longinus, 'On the Sublime,' Demetrius,'On Style.'* Trans. Stephen Halliwell. Cambridge, MA: Harvard University Press, 1995.

Armstrong, Philip. *Shakespeare in Psychoanalysis.* New York: Routledge, 2001.

Arnold, Matthew. 'Preface to the First Edition of *Poems.*' Kenneth Allot, ed. *The Poems of Matthew Arnold.* 1st ed. London: Longman, 1969.

Attie, Katherine Bootle. 'Passion Turned to Prettiness: Rhyme or Reason in *Hamlet.*' *Shakespeare Quarterly* 63.3 (2012): 393–423.

Auden, W. H. *Lectures on Shakespeare.* Arthur Kirsch, ed. Princeton: Princeton University Press, 2000.

Bacon, Sir Francis. 'Of Revenge.' *The essays, or councils, civil and moral, of Sir Francis Bacon, Lord Verulam, Viscount St. Alban.* London, 1696. Wing / B296.

Beer, Barrett L. *Tudor England Observed: The World of John Stow.* Gloucestershire: Sutton Publishing, 1998.

Belsey, Catherine. *Shakespeare and the Loss of Eden: The Construction of Family Values in Early Modern Culture*. New Brunswick, NJ: Rutgers University Press, 1999.

—'Shakespeare's Sad Tale for Winter: *Hamlet* and the Tradition of Fireside Ghost Stories.' *Shakespeare Quarterly* 61.1 (2010): 1–27.

Bevington, David. *Murder Most Foul: Hamlet Through the Ages*. New York: Oxford University Press, 2011.

Boehrer, Bruce Thomas. *Monarchy and Incest in Renaissance England: Literature, Culture, Kinship, and Kingship*. Philadelphia: University of Pennsylvania Press, 1992.

Booth, Stephen. 'On the value of Hamlet.' *Reinterpretations of Elizabethan Drama: Selected Papers from the English Institute*. Ed. Norman Rabkin. New York: Columbia University Press, 1969. 137–76.

Bradley, A. C. *Shakespearean Tragedy: Lectures on Hamlet, Othello, King Lear, Macbeth*. 2nd edn. New York: St. Martin's Press, 1978.

Bristol, Michael D. *Carnival and Theater: Plebeian Culture and the Structure of Authority in Renaissance England*. New York: Methuen, 1985.

—'The Customary and the Ethical: Understanding Hamlet's Bad Habits.' *Shakespeare Studies* 40 (2012): 70–6.

Burke, Peter. *Popular Culture in Early Modern Europe*. 3rd edn. Burlington, VT: Ashgate, 2009.

Bushnell, Rebecca. *Tragedy: A Short Introduction*. Malden, MA: Blackwell, 2008.

Callaghan, Dympna. *Shakespeare Without Women: Representing Gender and Race on the Renaissance Stage*. New York: Routledge, 2000.

—*Shakespeare's Sonnets*. Malden, MA: Wiley-Blackwell, 2008.

—*Who Was William Shakespeare?* Malden, MA: Wiley-Blackwell, 2013.

—ed. *A Feminist Companion to Shakespeare*. Malden, MA: Wiley-Blackwell, 2001.

—*The Impact of Feminism in English Renaissance Studies*. New York: Palgrave Macmillan, 2007.

Cantor, Paul A. *Shakespeare: Hamlet: A Student Guide*. 2nd edn. Cambridge: Cambridge University Press, 2004.

Cardullo, Robert J. 'The Delay of Polonius in Shakespeare's Hamlet.' *Neophilologus* 96.3 (2012): 487–95.

Cheney, Patrick, ed. *The Cambridge Companion to Christopher Marlowe*. Cambridge: Cambridge University Press, 2004.

Cicero, Marcus Tullius. *Cicero on Oratory and Orators*. J. S. Watson ed. and trans. Carbondale, IL: South Illinois University Press, 1986.

Clover, Carol J. *Men, Women, and Chainsaws: Gender in the Modern Horror Film*. Princeton: Princeton University Press, 1992.

Colclough, David. *Freedom of Speech in Early Stuart England*. Cambridge: Cambridge University Press, 2009.

Coleridge, Samuel Taylor. 'Notes on Hamlet.' In *The Complete Works of Samuel Taylor Coleridge*. ed. William Greenough Thayer Shedd. Vol. IV. New York: Harper & Brothers, 1853.

Conklin, Paul S. *A History of Hamlet Criticism 1601–1821*. London: Routledge & Kegan Paul, 1947.

Coyle, Martin, ed. *Hamlet: New Casebooks*. Basingstoke: Palgrave Macmillan, 1992.

Cressy, David. *Literacy and the Social Order: Reading and Writing in Tudor and Stuart England*. Cambridge: Cambridge University Press, 2006.

Crewe, Jonathan. 'Reading Horatio.' *Shakespeare Quarterly* 62.2 (2011): 271–8.

Critchley, Simon and Jamieson Webster. *Stay, Illusion!: the Hamlet Doctrine*. Pantheon: New York, 2013.

Crowther, John, ed. 'No Fear Hamlet.' SparkNotes.com. SparkNotes LLC.2005.Web.2 September 2014.

Crystal, David. *Think On My Words: Exploring Shakespeare's Language*. Cambridge: Cambridge University Press, 2008.

Crystal, David and Ben Crystal. *The Shakespeare Miscellany*. New York: Penguin, 2005.

David, Lloyd, ed. *Shakespeare Matters: History, Teaching, Performance*. Cranbury, NJ: Associated University Presses, 2003.

Davies, Michael. *Hamlet: Character Studies*. New York: Continuum, 2008.

Dawson, Anthony. *Shakespeare in Performance: Hamlet*. Manchester: Manchester University Press, 1995.

Descartes, René. *Discourse on Method, Optics, Geometry, and Meteorology*. Trans. Paul J. Olscamp. Rev. edn. Indianapolis: Hackett Publishing, 2001.

Deutermann, Allison K. ' "Caviare to the general"?: Taste, Hearing, and Genre in *Hamlet*.' *Shakespeare Quarterly* 62.2 (2011): 230–55.

Dolan, Frances E. 'Taking the Pencil Out of God's Hand: Art, Nature, and the Face-Painting Debate in Early Modern England.' *PMLA* 108.2 (1993): 224–39.

—*Dangerous Familiars: Representations of Domestic Crime in England, 1550–1700*. Ithaca, NY: Cornell University Press, 1994.

—*Whores Of Babylon: Catholicism, Gender And Seventeenth-Century Print Culture*. Notre Dame, IN: University of Notre Dame Press, 2005.

—*Marriage and Violence: The Early Modern Legacy*. Philadelphia: University of Pennsylvania Press, 2011.

Edelman, Lee. 'Against Survival: Queerness in a Time That's Out of Joint.' *Shakespeare Quarterly* 62.2 (2011): 148–69.

Eliot, T. S. 'Hamlet and his problems.' *The Sacred Wood: Essays on Poetry and Criticism*. 2nd edn. London: Methuen, 1928, 95–103.

Engle, Lars. 'Moral Agency in *Hamlet*.' *Shakespeare Studies* 40 (2012): 87–97.

—'How Is Horatio Just?: How Just is Horatio?' *Shakespeare Quarterly* 62.2 (2011): 256–62.

Farabee, Darlene. *Shakespeare's Staged Spaces and Playgoers' Perceptions*. London: Palgrave Macmillan, 2014.

Foakes, R. A. 'Hamlet's Neglect of Revenge.' *Hamlet: New Critical Essays*. ed. Arthur F. Kinney. New York: Routledge, 2002. 85–99.

—*Shakespeare and Violence*. Cambridge: Cambridge University Press, 2003.

Freccero, Carla. 'Forget Hamlet.' *Shakespeare Quarterly* 62.2 (2011): 170–3.

Freud, Sigmund. *The Freud Reader*. Ed. Peter Gay. New York: W. W. Norton, 1989.

Frye, Roland Mushat. *The Renaissance Hamlet: Issues and Responses in 1600*. Princeton, NJ: Princeton University Press, 1984.

Garber, Marjorie. ' "The Rest is Silence": Ineffability and the "Unscene" in Shakespeare's Plays.' *Ineffability: Naming the Unnamable from Dante to Beckett*. Eds. Peter S. Hawkins and Anne Howland Schotter. New York: AMS Press, 1984, 35–50.

—'A Tale of Three Hamlets: or, Repetition and Revenge.' *Shakespeare Quarterly* 61.1 (2010): 28–55.

Giddens, Eugene. *How to Read a Shakespearean Play Text.* Cambridge: Cambridge University Press, 2011.

Grady, Hugh. '*Hamlet* as mourning-play.' *Shakespeare and Impure Aesthetics.* Cambridge: Cambridge University Press, 2009, 133–92.

de Grazia, Margreta. *Hamlet Without Hamlet.* Cambridge: Cambridge University Press, 2007.

Greenblatt, Stephen. *Hamlet in Purgatory.* Princeton, NJ: Princeton University Press, 2002.

—*Will in the World: How Shakespeare Became Shakespeare.* New York: W. W. Norton, 2004.

Greenblatt, Stephen and Peter G. Platt, eds. *Shakespeare's Montaigne: The Florio Translation of the Essays: A Selection.* New York: New York Review of Books, 2014.

Greene, Roland, Stephen Cushman, Clare Cavanagh, et al., eds. *The Princeton Encyclopedia of Poetry and Poetics.* 4th edn. Princeton, NJ: Princeton University Press, 2011.

Hanson, Elizabeth. 'Fellow Students: Hamlet, Horatio, and the Early Modern University.' *Shakespeare Quarterly* 62.2 (2011): 205–29.

Harris, Jonathan Gil. 'From the Editor: Surviving *Hamlet*.' *Shakespeare Quarterly* 62.2 (2011): 145–7.

Hawkins, Peter S. and Anne Howland Schotter, eds. *Ineffability: Naming the Unnamable from Dante to Beckett.* New York: AMS Press, 1984.

Hazlitt, William. *Characters of Shakespeare's Plays.* London: C. H. Reynell, 1817.

Helgerson, Richard. *Forms of Nationhood: The Elizabethan Writing of England.* Chicago: University of Chicago Press, 1992.

Henderson, Katherine Usher and Barbara F. McManus, eds. *Half Humankind: Contexts & Texts of the Controversy about Women in England, 1540–1640.* Urbana: University of Illinois Press, 1985.

Howard, Jean E. *Shakespeare's Art of Orchestration: Stage Technique and Audience Response.* Urbana: University of Illinois Press, 1984.

Howard, Tony. *Women as Hamlet: Performance and Interpretation in Theatre, Film and Fiction.* Cambridge: Cambridge University Press, 2009.

Hunt, Marvin W. *Looking for Hamlet*. New York: Palgrave Macmillan, 2007.

Jones, Ernest. *Hamlet and Oedipus*. New York: Doubleday, 1954.

Jonson, Ben. *Discoveries*. Ed. Ian Donaldson. New York: Oxford University Press, 1985.

Jowett, John. *Shakespeare and Text*. Oxford: Oxford University Press, 2007.

Karim-Cooper, Farah. *Cosmetics in Shakespearean and Renaissance Drama*. Edinburgh: University of Edinburgh Press, 2006.

Karlyn, Kathleen Rowe. *Unruly Girls, Unrepentant Mothers: Redefining Feminism on Screen*. Austin: University of Texas Press, 2011.

Kerrigan, John. *Revenge Tragedy: Aeschylus to Armageddon*. Oxford: Clarendon Press, 1996.

Kinney, Arthur F., ed. *Hamlet: New Critical Essays*. New York: Routledge, 2002.

Kliman, Bernice W. 'Print and Electronic Editions Inspired by the New Variorum Hamlet Project.' *Shakespeare Survey*. Vol. 59: Editing Shakespeare. Ed. Peter Holland. Cambridge: Cambridge University Press, 2006, 157–67.

—'At Sea about Hamlet at Sea: A Detective Story.' *Shakespeare Quarterly* 62.2 (2011): 180–204.

Knight, Wilson. *The Wheel of Fire*. Oxford: Oxford University Press, 1930.

Lanham, Richard A. *The Motives of Eloquence: Literary Rhetoric in the Renaissance*. New Haven: Yale University Press, 1976.

Lawrence, D. H. *Complete Poems*. Eds. Vivian de Sola Pinto and Warren F. Roberts. New York: Penguin, 1993.

Lees-Jeffries, Hester. *Shakespeare and Memory*. Oxford: Oxford University Press, 2013.

Leinwand, Theodore. '*Hamlet's* Alchemy: Response to Katherine Eggert.' *Shakespeare Quarterly* 64.1 (2013): 58–9.

Lever, J. W. *The Tragedy of State*. London: Methuen, 1971.

Lewis, C. S. 'Hamlet: The Prince or The Poem?' *C. S. Lewis: Selected Literary Essays*. Ed. Walter Hooper. Cambridge: Cambridge University Press, 1969, 88–105.

Lewis, Rhodri. 'Hamlet, Metaphor, and Memory.' *Studies in Philology* 109.5 (2012): 609–41.

Lima, Robert. *Stages of Evil: Occultism in Western Theater and Drama*. Lexington, KY: The University Press of Kentucky, 2005.

Marlowe, Christopher. *The Complete Works of Christopher Marlowe*. Vol. 1. Ed. Fredson Bowers. 2nd edn. Cambridge: Cambridge University Press, 1981.

Maus, Katharine Eisaman, ed. *Four Revenge Tragedies: The Spanish Tragedy, The Revenger's Tragedy, The Revenge of Bussy D'Ambois, and The Atheist's Tragedy*. New York: Oxford University Press, 1995.

McEachern, Claire. *The Cambridge Companion to Shakespearean Tragedy*. Cambridge: Cambridge University Press, 2013.

McEvoy, Sean. *Shakespeare: The Basics*. 3rd edn. New York: Routledge, 2012.

Melchiori, Giorgio. '*Hamlet*: The Acting Version and the Wiser Sort.' *The Hamlet First Published (Q1, 1603): Origins, Form, Intertextualities*. Ed. Thomas Clayton. Newark, NJ: University of Delaware Press, 1992. 195–210.

Menzer, Paul. *The Hamlets: Cues, Qs, and Remembered Texts*. Cranbury, NJ: Associated University Presses, 2010.

Murphy, Andrew. *The Renaissance Text: Theory, Editing, Textuality*. Manchester: Manchester University Press, 2000.

Nashe, Thomas. *The Unfortunate Traveller and Other Works*. ed. J. B. Steane, New York: Penguin, 1985.

Newell, Alex. *The Soliloquies in Hamlet: The Structural Design*. Cranbury, NJ: Associated University Presses, 1991.

Newman, Karen. 'Two Lines, Three Readers: *Hamlet*, TLN 1904-5.' *Shakespeare Quarterly* 62.2 (2011): 263–70.

Nicholas, Nick and Andrew Strader, trans. *Khamlet: Hamlet, Prince of Denmark: The Restored Klingon Version*. Ed. Mark Shoulson. Flourtown, PA: Klingon Language Institute, 1996.

Orgel, Stephen and Sean Keilen, eds. *Shakespeare and the Editorial Tradition: The Scholarly Literature*. New York: Routledge, 1999.

Ovid. *Ovid's Metamorphoses*. Trans. Charles Martin. New York: W. W. Norton, 2005.

Palfrey, Simon. *Doing Shakespeare*. London: Bloomsbury, 2005; 2011.

Paolucci, Anne. 'Bradley and Hegel on Shakespeare.' *Comparative Literature*. 16.3 (1964): 211–25.

Parker, Patricia. *Literary Fat Ladies: Rhetoric, Gender, Property*. London: Methuen, 1987.

Paster, Gail Kern. 'Thinking with Skulls in Holbein, *Hamlet*, Vesalius, and Fuller.' *The Shakespearean International Yearbook*. Vol. 11: *Placing Michael Neill: Issues of Space and Place in Shakespeare and Early Modern Culture*. Eds. Graham Bradshaw, Tom Bishop, Alexander C. Y. Huang, and Jonathan Gil Harris. Farnham: Ashgate, 2011, 41–60.

Peltonen, Markku. *Rhetoric, Politics and Popularity in Pre-Revolutionary England*. Cambridge: Cambridge University Press, 2013.

Pollard, Tanya. 'What's Hecuba to Shakespeare?' *Renaissance Quarterly* 65.4 (2012): 1060–93.

Potter, Lois. *The Life of William Shakespeare: A Critical Biography*. Malden, MA: Wiley-Blackwell, 2012.

Prose, Francine. *Reading Like a Writer: A Guide for People Who Love Books and for Those Who Want to Write Them*. London: Aurum Press, 2012.

Raleigh, W. A., S. Lee, and C. T. Onions. *Shakespeare's England*, Vol. 1. Oxford: Clarendon Press, 1916.

Rosenberg, Marvin. *The Masks of Hamlet*. Newark, NJ: University of Delaware Press, 1992.

Rothwell, Kenneth S. *A History of Shakespeare on Screen: A Century of Film and Television*. 2nd edn. Cambridge: Cambridge University Press, 2004.

Schalkwyk, David. *Hamlet's Dreams: The Robben Island Shakespeare*. London: Bloomsbury, 2012.

Schoen, Lawrence. *The Klingon Hamlet: The Restored Edition—Prepared by the Klingon Language Institute*. New York: Pocket Books, 2000.

Schwarz, Kathryn. '*Hamlet* without Us.' *Shakespeare Quarterly* 62.2 (2011): 174–9.

Shaughnessy, Robert. ed. *The Cambridge Companion to Shakespeare and Popular Culture*. Cambridge: Cambridge University Press, 2007.

—'*Hamlet*.' *The Routledge Guide to William Shakespeare*. New York: Routledge, 2011, 190–202.

Stanton, Kay. *Shakespeare's 'Whores': Erotics, Politics, and Poetics*. New York: Palgrave Macmillan, 2014.

States, Bert O. *Hamlet and the Concept of Character*. Baltimore: Johns Hopkins University Press, 1992.

Stern, Tiffany. *Documents of Performance in Early Modern England*. Cambridge: Cambridge University Press, 2009.

Tandon, Bharat. 'Victorian Shakespeares.' *The Oxford Handbook of Victorian Poetry*. Matthew Bevis, ed. New York: Oxford University Press, 2013. 201–16.

Taylor, A. B., ed. *Shakespeare's Ovid: The Metamorphoses in the Plays and Poems*. Cambridge: Cambridge University Press, 2000.

Taylor, George Coffin. *Shakespeare's Debt to Montaigne*. Cambridge: Harvard University Press, 1925.

Tobin, J. J. M. '*Hamlet* and Nashe's *Lenten Stuffe*.' *Archiv* 219 (1982): 388–95.

Vallance, Edward. *Revolutionary England and the National Covenant: State Oaths, Protestantism and the Political Nation, 1553–1682*. Rochester, NY: Boydell Press, 2005.

Weimann, Robert. 'Mimesis in Hamlet.' In *Shakespeare and the Question of Theory*. Eds. Patricia Parker and Geoffrey Hartman. New York: Methuen, 1985, 275–91.

—*Author's Pen and Actor's Voice: Playing and Writing in Shakespeare's Theatre*. Cambridge: Cambridge University Press, 2000.

Werstine, Paul. 'The Textual Mystery of *Hamlet*.' *Shakespeare Quarterly* 39 (1988): 1–26.

White, R. S. 'Ophelia's Sisters.' *The Impact of Feminism in English Renaissance Studies*. ed. Dympna Callaghan. New York: Palgrave Macmillan, 2007, 93–113.

Wilson, Thomas. *The Arte of Rhetorique*. London, 1553. STC (2nd edn) / 25799.

Worthen, W. B. *Shakespeare and the Authority of Performance*. Cambridge: Cambridge University Press, 1997.

Wright, George T. 'Hendiadys and Hamlet.' *PMLA* 96.2 (1981): 168–93.

—*Shakespeare's Metrical Art*. Berkeley: University of California Press, 1988.

Editions of the play

Bertram, Paul and Bernice Kliman, eds. *The Three-text Hamlet: Parallel Texts of the First and Second Quartos and the First Folio*. New York: AMS Press, 1991.

Greenblatt, Stephen, et al., eds. *The Norton Shakespeare*. New York: W. W. Norton, 1997.

Himan, Charlton, ed. *The Norton Facsimile: The First Folio of Shakespeare*. 2nd edn. New York: W. W. Norton, 1996.

Shakespeare, William. *Hamlet*. The Arden Shakespeare. Second Series. Harold Jenkins, ed. London: Methuen, 1982.

Shakespeare, William. *Hamlet*. The Arden Shakespeare. Third Series. Ann Thompson and Neil Taylor, eds. London: Thomson, 2007.

Shakespeare, William. *Hamlet: The Texts of 1603 and 1623*. The Arden Shakespeare. Third Series. Ann Thompson and Neil Taylor, eds. London: Methuen, 2006.

Shakespeare, William. *Hamlet*. A Norton Critical Edition. Robert S. Miola, ed. New York: W. W. Norton, 2010.

Films

Hamlet. Directed by Gregory Doran. 2009. Made for British television by BBC Productions in association with Illuminations and the Royal Shakespeare Company.

Hamlet. Directed by Michael Almereyda. 2000. double A Films.

Hamlet. Directed by Kenneth Branagh. 1996. Castle Rock Entertainment, Turner Pictures (I) and Fishmonger Films.

Hamlet. Directed by Franco Zeffirelli, starring Mel Gibson. 1990. Warner Bros.

Hamlet. Directed by Grigori Kozintsev. 1964. Lenfilm.

Hamlet. Directed by Laurence Olivier. 1948. Two Cities Films.

Theatrical performances

Klingon Performance: http://www.youtube.com/
    watch?v=CiRMGYQfXrs
Laurence Olivier's *Hamlet* performance: http://www.youtube.com/
    watch?v=ARd8aORVyoQ
Royal Shakespeare Company Performance Database: http://www.
    rsc.org.uk/about-us/history/performance-database.aspx

Websites

The Bodleian First Folio: (http://firstfolio.bodleian.ox.ac.uk).
Concordance of Shakespeare's Complete Works: (http://www.
    opensourceshakespeare.org/concordance/).
Digital Folger: (http://www.folger.edu/Content/Whats-On/
    Digital-Folger/).
Drama Online: (http://www.dramaonlinelibrary.com/).
Hamlet on the Ramparts: (http://shea.mit.edu/ramparts/).
Hamlet Works: (hamletworks.org).
Internet Shakespeare Editions: (http://internetshakespeare.uvic.ca/
    Library/facsimile/).
Shakespeare On Screen: (http://www.screenonline.org.uk/film/
    id/444972/index.html).
Shakespeare's Words: (http://www.shakespeareswords.com).